POP

by

Domenico Martino

Edited by Dr. Rocco Leonard Martino

BLUENOSE PRESS
WWW.BLUENOSEPRESS.COM

A Division of Chesapeake Bay Media, LLC

Please visit: www.bluenosepress.com

Published by:

BlueNose Press, Inc.
A Division of Chesapeake Bay Media, LLC
Printed in the United States of America
Published February, 2016

Works by Rocco Leonard Martino

Fiction

The Cross of Victory
Christianity: A Criminal Investigation...
The Resurrection: A Criminal Investigation...
9-11-11: The Tenth Anniversary Attack
The Plot to Cancel Christmas

Radio Drama

X the Unknown: There is no Christ in Christmas

Nonfiction

Memories: Volume I - Stories for My Grandchildren
Memories: Volume II - Scientist and Writer
Memories: Volume III - Changing the World
Rocket Ships and God
Walking Around the Neighborhood
People, Machines, and Politics of the Cyber Age Creation
Essays Along the Way
Finding the Critical Path
Applied Operational Planning
Allocating and Scheduling Resources
Critical Path Networks
Resources Management
Dynamic Costing
Project Management
Decision Patterns

Decision Tables with Staff of MDI
Information Management
Integrated Manufacturing Systems
Management Information Systems
MIS Methodology
Personnel Management Systems
Computer-R-Age with Webster V. Allen
IMPACT 70s with John Gentile
UNIVAC Operations Manual
Ground Effect of Radio Wave Propagation
Heat Transfer in Slip Flow

DEDICATION

"Pop did not create a Dedication Page for this book. It would be presumptuous for me to do so now. But I can speculate. To whom would Pop have dedicated the autobiography of his life? But of course, 'To family!'"

Rocco Leonard Martino
Villanova, Pennsylvania
February 15th, 2016

FOREWARD

In 1980, I originally wanted to help my father publish this book, but delayed its completion until now for a number of reasons. "Pop" became ill and died in December of 1982. Since then, time and business constraints made it impossible for me to pursue the publication of his autobiography until now. With the passage of time has come the awareness of the need to bring Pop to the public.

I feel privileged in writing the Preface for "Pop." This book is the story of Domenico Martino, a young immigrant boy, who- though he did not find the streets paved with the proverbial gold of the New World- did indeed find a land of opportunity, adventure, growth, and ultimately, a new homeland. Pop's story spans two continents, the beginning of a new century, two world wars and includes reminiscences of the hinterland of Canada. As Pop neared his 80th birthday, he looked back over the years- years marked with joy and tragedy, success and failure, and the normal vicissitudes encountered by all of us. What makes his story more poignant, however, are the anecdotes, observations, and down-to-earth approach that color his philosophy of life with a warmth that is the real mark of a unique person giving us the benefit of his life experience.

I am proud of this man, proud of all I have learned from him, and proud of the fact I have been privileged above all else to call him "Pop". The title of this book could not be anything else.

With the exception of some editing and the occasional comment from me, this book is Pop. The following chapters contain his thoughts, his words, and most importantly, his outlook on life. I hope that you, the reader, will find his story as absorbing as I have in hearing and seeing and living some of it.

Rocco Leonard Martino
Villanova, Pennsylvania
February 15th, 2016

TABLE OF CONTENTS

Preface   1

Introduction   9

Chapter 1: Looking Back to the Beginning
  o Modugno   11
  o Growing Up   21
  o Life and Death in Italy   31

Chapter 2: Off to America
  o The New World Beckons   37
  o Canada   45

Chapter 3: Life in a New Country
  o Adjusting to Change   59
  o Teenage Adventures   71

Chapter 4: Learning About Life
  o After the War   89
  o Appreciating Differences   106
  o Going Home   111

Chapter 5: Settling Down
  o Challenges in America:
    Starting a Family   117
  o The Great Depression   131
  o Losing a Wife   138

Chapter 6: The Middle Years
  o Raising Sons Alone   143
  o Another War   149
  o Starting Over   155

Chapter 7: The Reflective Years
    o   Being a Grandfather   167
    o   Time to Relax and Think   175
    o   Facing Your Own Mortality 184

Epilogue: Aunt Mary's Trip to America   205

Appendix A: Pop's Obituary   209

Appendix B: The Silver Rail   213

Appendix C: The Silver Goblet Award   215

PREFACE

I always remember my father whistling while he worked. Sometimes, he even did a little jig as he whistled. Whether in the restaurant as he planned to feed hundreds, or at home planning a sumptuous meal for me alone, Pop whistled.

Pop was a Master Chef. After arriving from his native Italy, he settled in Toronto with his father in 1914. As a young man, he traveled across the country working in hotels, lumber camps, and restaurants. In his late twenties, he began to study hard to become the superb artist and culinary craftsman I grew up to know. Pop was an author, a culinary judge, and respected and loved by all who knew him or of him. He also devoted his spare time to children, especially the sick, the crippled, and the incurable.

He was always happy no matter what he did. He lived in the present with an eye to the future, but only to life's storms, needs, and uncertainties. His philosophy was not one of being sad today to be happy tomorrow. He experienced enough sadness in his lifetime to "appreciate the moment" and take advantage of the small daily happiness life has to offer whenever he could.

My fondest memories of him are in the kitchen-the aroma of good food prepared with a whistle and a smile. Pop spoiled me rotten when it came to food. After I moved to Philadelphia, whenever I returned home to Toronto, he created a superb banquet for two. We laughed, joked, talked, and just had fun. Dinner lasted hours. Pop liked to do this little jig, especially when he had decorated some dish to artistic perfection. He always talked of "the appeal of the eye", and how it magnified taste. He felt dining was necessary for both the body and the spirit. He loved his work, and took pleasure in making people happy.

Pure and simple, Pop took joy in being alive- in his work, and in the people around him. Pop whistled to the canary, at the canary, and with the canary. He talked to people on trains, streetcars, and restaurants. When he ate out, he always complimented the chef on a good meal. And he always did it as a fellow professional to add extra meaning to the compliment.

Pop was a naturally happy man. He was born in Modugno, a small Italian village along the Adriatic. His father was a wine merchant, who often took his young son with him as he made the rounds of the local vineyards. Pop's mother was the educated daughter of a major landowner; an excellent accountant, she kept the books for her husband's business. She was also an equally excellent cook and it was from her that Pop learned to cook with an appeal to all the senses.

When the world-wide Depression of 1911 hit the little town of Modugno, my grandfather decided to investigate wine-making possibilities in Toronto. After much coaxing, he reluctantly agreed to take Pop with him for what they both thought would be a short visit. As father and son left, Pop's grandfather hugged them and said, "Please don't go; you'll never come back; I'll never see you again." His words were prophetic, for four months later Pop's father- who was concerned about a sick son at home- returned to Italy leaving my fourteen year old father in the care of an uncle. Unfortunately, World War I broke out, and it would be a long time before Pop and my grandfather would see each other again.

Pop grew up without his father or mother with him through adolescence, the first Great War, and the dreadful post-war Spanish flu epidemic. During the epidemic, Pop helped a missionary from China administer to the ill. This post-war experience and the searing memory of returning veterans, scarred and maimed for life, would haunt my father forever.

Like many boys of his generation, Pop wanted an excuse to drop out of school and the shoe shining business provided such an excuse. But he soon tired of this work and turned to a job that would provide him not only with an income, but a career and reputation for the rest of his life- cooking. The pursuit of this career took him from the cities of Toronto, Ontario and Buffalo, New York, to far-flung outposts of Northern Canada, where he worked as a short order lumberjack cook.

Pop eventually saved enough money to return to Italy to see his parents. What a joyful reunion that was! But the visit was bittersweet. Pop had missed his parents terribly, last seen them as a thirteen year-old boy, and was now seeing them again as a twenty-three year old young man. The reality didn't gibe with his memories. I remember Pop telling me how surprised he was that the town was so dowdy and the buildings so small. The piazza that had grown so proudly in his memory was a dusty square in the center of town. After the initial assault of his memories, the joy of being with family again took over. That, for him, was always the key to life- the family was sacred, a community, a blanket to surround you with love to keep the hurt, the cold, and the dark out. With family, all was light, life, and comfort under any and all circumstances.

As the "successful American" returning home, Pop was the darling of the community. He dated, but had hardly gotten to know all the young ladies who had grown up in his absence, when he had to leave or face being drafted into the Italian army. So, Pop returned to America.

By this time, of course, he was a grown man ready to settle down and start a family of his own, which he did upon his return to Toronto. In 1925, Pop fell in love with and married a beautiful red-haired, green-eyed wonder, Josephine DiGiulio, the young and attractive daughter of a prosperous Toronto family.

Pop met my mother through a friend, my Uncle Donald. Donald DiGiulio bore a startling resemblance to images of Julius Caesar Pop had seen on coins and in books and Uncle Donald humorously propagated the myth that the DiGiulio's were direct descendants of Julius Caesar. The claim, of course, was completely without basis since no family records went back that far. But built around this point of camaraderie, the two became fast friends. All his life, Uncle Donald spoke of Pop as a man of humor and honor. For that reason he decided to introduce my father to his sister, Josephine.

The new couple's first son, Jack, was a joy, born on April 14, 1926, and was followed by a second in November of 1927. But these were the days before antibiotics and this second child died during a

4

diphtheria and whooping cough epidemic in 1929. I was born on June 25th of that same year. Being a parent myself, I can just imagine the anguish my mother and father went through at that time. Years later, Pop would often speak of my dead brother with a tear in his eye. Still, he drew strength at all times from the love from his family and his philosophy of facing tragedy with courage. Being a practical man, he also believed in moderation in all things. In this sense, tragedy had to be put in perspective and rapidly coped with because there was so much to live for.

I remember how content my father seemed when he was with his family. <u>We</u> were what Pop had to live for. Unlike some other men, Pop relished the responsibility of caring for and protecting his wife and children. I knew he loved my mother dearly. I knew he loved me and my brother. I remember the quiet things-playing ball together, picnics, family gatherings, dinners at home. I never saw my parents bicker or argue, nor did they ever lose their tempers with us. We all had a deep respect and caring for one another. Josephine (my mother) died tragically in 1938 after a miscarriage that resulted in recurrent hemorrhaging and a lengthy illness that caused her to become a shell of her former self. My father chose to raise us two boys alone; he refused to remarry because he felt stepmother relationships didn't work out. In fact, he waited until we were grown before he married again. At 75, Pop lost his second wife. In between, he fought to survive three heart attacks, increasing loss of vision and continuing problems with melanoma. Finally, he died at age 82.

My memories of Pop are always of a quiet, thoughtful man, highly intelligent, who lived in a world of people and family. The trappings of wealth were not important to him- he measured wealth in terms of love, not dollars. In the midst of the Great Depression of the 30's when he was making twenty-five dollars a week, whenever he visited his sister or brother he always gave each niece or nephew a dollar. He always felt it was his duty and his joy to be the "patriarch," the uncle. Everyone loved Pop, just as he too loved everyone in his large, extended family.

Two nights before Pop died, we had a long talk. We talked of politics, statesmen, the popes, of friends, placed he'd been all over Canada, his youth, and his life. Our four-hour talk ranged over the world, over decades. The whole time he smiled and his eyes were alive with pleasure. There were also some sad moments for him as we relived Mom's death.

He knew he was going to die, even if I would not accept it. I kept telling him he would be going home for Christmas, but he laughed and said, "You must be kidding!" Then he started to tire and in a quiet but strong voice, Pop told me what he wanted done. All his personal effects were to go to the poor; money to his grandchildren; and his home and love to my brother and me. He smiled and kissed us both good night.

The next day he was weak. We talked a little, but it was more a wave of his hand. But Pop still smiled. That was a Friday. It was December 10th and some well-known CBC (Canadian Broadcasting Company) personalities came to St. Margaret's Hospital to sing Christmas carols. He said he was too tired to have his bed wheeled in, but he told me to go while he napped. That night, we talked a little and softly.

On Saturday afternoon, Pop died sitting in a chair beside his bed, wrapped in smiling sunlight. Death had been swift yet gentle- an enormous pulmonary embolism…just a massive sigh. The smile and the whistle were gone. My brother Jack and I sat with him after the nurses returned him to his bed; it was peaceful. That night we planned his funeral.

The <u>Toronto Star</u> had carried a long obituary about Pop on the day before his funeral; the Church was full of many friends who came to say farewell to this good man. The funeral itself was a blend of glory and sadness. All the pews were filled. The music fit my father's life": The spiritual "Prayer of St. Francis", the "Our Father", the "Ave Maria", and the joyous hymn, "On Eagles Wings". There was also the grandeur of "Faith of Our Fathers"- sung with a celebratory ring of having "kept the faith". Afterwards, all the family gathered for lunch. Uncle Mike- my father's only surviving brother- who was then in his seventies, summed it up in a quiet, thoughtful way: "The old boy sure knew how to live!"

Posthumously on January 10, 1983, I flew back to Toronto to accept an award for my father. Jack insisted I accept the award because I had worked so closely with Pop on his books and in his charitable work at the hospitals. He was honored as Man of the Year for his humanitarian work. It was Canada's Silver Cup Award, which I cherish to this day. My brother and I were happy for Pop. He had lived a full life, and was content and satisfied when he died- which is all any of us can really ask for. Throughout his life, Pop never sought honors or returns on what he did for others from his heart. This award was final recognition of the goodness and value of his life. For that, we were happy. Our one regret was that Pop himself would never know he was the recipient of this great honor.

On the night of the award, and forever after, Jack and I both heard the whistling in our minds and in our hearts, saw him tighten his apron, tilt his chef's hat, and lift his teacup in a final sip before going to serve his guests for lunch.

Pop continues to whistle.

INTRODUCTION

Most people my age are either dead or parked in a corner waiting to die. But I'm not! I was born in 1900 and I'll be around to celebrate the turn of the century- either that or I'll die trying.

It's hard to believe that I'm 80- hard because I don't feel like 80; but then again, what's 80 supposed to feel like? And hard because the 80 years seems to have passed so quickly. I'm the same person now that I was years ago, but every year I just move a little slower, and the winters get a little colder.

I don't resent being old, but I do resent the attitude that assumes I must be decrepit if I've been around so long. I live alone in my own house, I do my own cooking and I still think for myself. I think it's about time people my age were treated as real, and not ornaments to be paraded around on holidays on one hand, or discarded as wards of the state on the other. Thank God I have two sons who see it my way instead of being silly enough to insist I give up my independence. After all, many people my age have made tremendous contributions. George Bernard Shaw wrote his last play at 96; Leo XIII was Pope until 95; Konrad Adenauer masterminded the creation of the modern Germany during his 80's; and Winston

Churchill was re-elected Prime Minister of Great Britain at 80.

During my life, I've experienced tremendous good fortune. While some things happened that I didn't like or appreciate, by and large, God has been good to me and life has been interesting. But don't get the wrong idea; it hasn't been a bed of roses either. I lost two wives and two children, I've suffered three heart attacks, I had several serious financial reverses, and I've experienced blindness.

Still, I've been lucky. I'm alive. I'm well. I have lived a full life and can look back with joyful nostalgia on so many good things, so much fun, and so many fond memories of people. I feel life has been a success.

You've probably never heard my name before reading this book. I'm not famous, nor am I wealthy in dollars- although I wouldn't trade my true wealth for all the gold or oil in the world. That true wealth I speak of is my family, my children, and my freedom.

So now, at 80, I've decided to write this book. Why? Because I'm like you. A person. Nothing more, nothing less. I think you might be interested in what happened to me during my lifetime, what I learned along the way, and how I feel about things now. You might find some comfort in comparing notes with me and feel happier knowing someone else lived through the same problems and difficulties, and like you, survived them a better person. Besides, I had so much fun traveling through my life that I'd like to share the trip with you.

Domenico Martino
Toronto, Ontario
April 1980

CHAPTER ONE

LOOKING BACK TO THE BEGINNING
"MODUGNO"

My life began on July 7, 1900. Of course, I was there, but don't remember anything about it, not even the slap I must have gotten on my behind from the midwife who delivered me. I was the third child, but the first son of Jack and Domenica Martino. My father was a wine merchant and my mother the educated daughter of an important landowner in the area. My family lived on the Adriatic coast of Italy, in a little town of about 15,000 people called Modugno (see map). In 1900, it was a small, sleepy, residential community with little industry surrounded by the farms of the townspeople. The land was flat and fertile, with small streams flowing around the center of town. Life in Modugno was centered on family, church, and friendships among the townspeople, all of whom gathered frequently in the central piazza of town. Picnics, concerts, games and "strolling" were all parts of daily life. Every evening the piazza was full of people sitting on benches on all four sides of the square. Everyone talked to one another. People cared. Neighbors knew each other and all their family members. Living in Modugno meant to belong.

Life was simple and somewhat bucolic- a contrast to today's world of computers, supersonic aircraft, television and nuclear war. In 1900, life moved at a slower pace, especially in Modugno. In fact, my birth wasn't even registered until July 11th, giving rise to some uncertainty about my birth date until my mother told me quite firmly that it was July 7th. My earliest memories are of our farm and the good earth. Land gives us so much in return, despite the neglect and continual assumption of its fertility by many.

My father and I used to work side by side, even when I was very young. Papa was a successful wine merchant and cantina owner; in my early years, he had three cantinas and a number of vineyards. In some places, he also had olive trees with presses to make olive oil. We would make three rounds of each location, checking with the workmen at each one. I always wanted to help, even though I was small for my age. I loved my father and wanted his attention and love. (We were great pals and I wanted to keep it that way!) I see this same desire now in other young children, and I saw it with my own. I feel great sorrow when I see parents who don't understand this longing for affection and comradeship from their children. Just being with my father, no matter what we were doing, was important. It gave me a sense of comfort and security.

I was very fortunate. As the oldest son, I came to know Papa best. To his credit, as each of my brothers and sisters were born, my father tried to equalize his time with all of us. However, as is often the case with first born sons (especially in an old-world Italian family), our special bond had been struck early on. I was the third child. My older sisters Filomena and Angelina- in the usual custom of the day- spent time with Mother, helping with the housework, cooking at the cantina, and raising the younger children. My younger sister, Nicoletta, was born in 1902 and my oldest side-kick and friend for life, my brother Frank (or Francesco), was born in 1904.

My memories of Papa are always warm and tender. He was a gentle man, full of love and compassion. Nothing ever seemed to bother him yet I knew, like all people, he was often troubled by misfortune and tragedy. From him I learned always to draw strength from the family, to give rather than seek, and to be moderate in all things. Years later I learned that his nickname was Martino "Pas-a-pas" or Martino "One step". Papa always took one step at a time in life, much like the Chinese proverb about how a journey of a thousand miles takes place one step at a time.

Throughout my childhood, I saw my father share not only his time, but his love among all his children as equally as possible. It was obvious that he loved my mother dearly. Of course, in the tradition of the day, men played a dominant role, and women were expected to be subservient. But my parents did not totally follow that tradition. They were more of an equal partnership, working together with a common goal to live well and to raise a family. They were generations ahead of their time, believing in equality in an age when use of this word was limited to political tracts and rarely given real meaning in practice.

The Catholic religion was an important part of life in Modugno and of my parents. Their marriage even came about because of the Church. My father's uncle was the Archpriest of the Church in Modugno and his closest friend was a "Father Selci", whose sister was married to Domenic Trentadue. One day, Father Martino happened to introduce his nephew, Jiacomo, to Father Selci, who immediately thought of introducing him to his niece, Domenica Trentadue. Within a year the two friends jointly officiated at the wedding of their niece and nephew. Needless to say, throughout my boyhood in Modugno and forever afterwards, my view of the Church was that it was an extension of my family. The Church was an integral part of everyone's daily lives, not a mysterious external or "foreign" entity to which people paid lip service. The Church was a friend that offered comfort and security, and help in times of distress.

I remember one incident in particular when I was nine years old that brought me much closer to my father. There was a rare phenomenon occurring in Italy at the time: Haley's comet appeared in the skies nightly over southern and eastern Italy in the fall of 1909.

In those days, everything in nature was given some deep dark meaning, and the comet was interpreted as a sign that the end of the world was approaching. It was even predicted to occur on a specific day in September at 2:00 in the morning when the star would fall to the earth, burning away most of the world. Whatever escaped the star would be destroyed by earthquakes or tidal waves. Imagine the effect this kind of talk had on a nine year old boy! I would go to bed scared to death that I would never see the morning. It was never discussed in our home though, because Mama and Papa didn't believe anyone could foretell the future, nor did they believe in rumors or cults. They were comfortable in their faith and tradition, which was based on a conservative, down-to-earth approach to life.

I, personally, was skeptical about the whole thing and had to find out for myself- the hard way. Since I didn't know for sure what was true, I decided the best way was to simply observe. So, on the day that the world was to come to an end, I snuck out of the house at 1:30am. Everyone was sound asleep, so my adventure was a secret. I went downtown to the piazza, where a lot of adults were just standing around expecting something to happen. I, too, stood and waited- not afraid, but curious.

Nothing happened! At 3:00am, I finally went home, very happy that the world was safe. However, I didn't have as much luck entering the house as I did leaving. Papa caught me sneaking back through the door. I told him where I was and how scared I had been. Instead of getting angry, though, he held me tight and told me that if I was ever afraid again to come to him with my fears. From then on, I always did. Even later, when I was alone as a boy in Canada, just thinking of Papa's comforting words made the worst look that much better.

In his usual thoughtful and caring way, Papa was understanding and always tried to be the best parent he could. He wanted to comfort me, help me learn, prepare me for life and hopefully teach me to someday be the kind of loving father he was.

Our life was simple and we worked hard to survive. Although we were comfortable, there was no luxury. My family was large and naturally, everyone contributed. In total, we were eleven children, of whom eight survived to maturity, four boys and four girls. Disease took three of my sisters, two as teenagers. I'm certain today's medical care and antibiotics would have saved them.

We lived with life <u>and</u> death all around us. As a youth, one of my most tragic experiences was the death of my sister, Nicoletta. She died suddenly in 1910, just after her First Communion. At first, she had a sore throat. Then a burning fever. In less than a week she was dead. I was ten, she was eight. We all cried, but my brother Frank and I probably cried hardest because the three of us had grown up together. Nicoletta's death made me realize at a young age that everyone is mortal. I feel that my living with a realistic and accepting view of death has helped me to truly appreciate life and live it to the fullest. Death will come soon enough, so there is no point in being dead while you're still breathing.

Growing up in the early 20th century with no miracle drugs, no trauma centers, no paramedics, and no medical insurance gave us a sense of truly being on our own. There was one doctor in town, but doctors were expensive, so none of us ever went to see him unless we were seriously ill. (Besides, doctors in those days couldn't do much anyway with the primitive medicine available to them.) As a result, my family- and everyone in Modugno- treated health, sickness, and death as distinct but normal phases of life, each to be dealt with in a different way. However, while medicine was primitive with regard to science and technology, it was rich in terms of the spirit. The sick were given love and courtesy. Today, in our attempts to prolong life, we often ignore its spiritual needs. While physicians try to save our bodies, our spirits are often crushed. Intensive Care Units for the seriously ill and dying should be beautiful rooms full of flowers and sunlight, with music playing and the laughter of living easing the fears and pain of the deathly sick. I have always believed it is far better to die in the dignity and quiet of your own home than in some noisy, dingy Intensive Care Unit. I have been in several of those, and I prayed in all cases to just get out so I could live or die in peace!

Death in the early 1900's was always waiting for the unwary or the sickly. People were careful not to get sick, but if you were, you knew friends, family, and God would help you get better as rapidly as possible. The emphasis was on staying healthy and recovering quickly. Still, we were careful by doing all things in moderation. People exercised, ate good food, worked, laughed, and loved with our friends and families. Without today's variety of stress factors, fast-paced lifestyles, and isolated families, we were able to relax and just live! Modern medicine is just re-discovering the benefits of this "old-fashioned" lifestyle now. I don't believe I ever heard the term "psychosomatic illness" used in Modugno. Illness was always of the body and not of the mind or psyche. I also never heard of anyone having a nervous breakdown- I suppose because everybody was too busy working at living and surviving to have time to get depressed.

EDITOR'S NOTE: The close-knit family and community relationships of the day certainly contributed to this "wellness" factor, particularly in regard to mental health. Knowing you had family and a variety of other support networks to turn to must have been a tremendous source of strength for everyone.

Both my parents worked hard to raise our family. They gave everything to either their children or their own parents. They lived by the time honored Italian code of selflessness and dedication to the truly important things of life- family, religion, and country...in that order. This code is epitomized by a story Papa told me that had been passed down through generations of the Martino family. The story goes that a man earned three coins a day and with it, he took care of the present, the past and the future. One coin paid his debt to the past, taking care of parents and grandparents on both sides; one coin went for the present, taking care of the expenses of the day- food, housing, and so on; and the final coin was invested in the future- caring for the children.

> EDITOR'S NOTE: This is an interesting insight into Italian culture, as well as the tradition of our family. I often heard Pop tell this story. I, in turn, tell it to my four sons. I believe a form of this tradition applies to all families, but is especially important in ours.

Both my parents lived this code throughout their lives. I lived it, and my two sons are living it the way they take care of both me and their own children. The great joy of my life is to know that I have succeeded in passing on to my children the tradition passed on to me by my parents.

My father was a very kind man, perhaps too kind by some standards. He trusted people- believing them, helping them when they needed it, never demanding, but always wanting to help. Of course, when it came to family, no sacrifice was too great. I often remember him reaching into his pocket for some coins. Then, as he handed them to me, he'd tell me to buy flowers, cakes, or fruit and take them to his parents. Everyday, I saw both sets of grandparents for as long as they were alive. This closeness created an awareness of family ties- and obligations- for me. Parents should not be ignored, cast away or placed in nursing home parking lots awaiting death. After my paternal grandmother died, my father often sent me to stay for a day or two with his father whenever he seemed lonely. Later, I went to live with him. As "Domenico", and as the oldest grandson, I was a special joy to my grandfather. The Italian tradition was to name children after their grandparents. Hence, I was Domenico for my grandfather, and my first son was Jiacomo for my own father.

My mother was just as kind as Papa, but different in many ways. Her kitchen was always one of delightful aromas. She was a perfectionist in her cooking, concentrating on taste, aroma, and presentation- lessons I learned from her that have carried me through my own career with cooking.

Mama always had a smile. Her life of partnership- both in business and family affairs- with my father led to her having her own individual responsibilities. She was strong and intelligent. Though she had the primary responsibility of raising us, Papa took over when it came to teaching his sons to work and act like men. Mama was the nurturing glue that held the family together. Thank God neither of them believed in corporal punishment. No matter what I did, I was never cuffed or slapped though I'm sure many times I came close! In fact, there were times when I would have preferred a quick slap on the bottom instead of the long lecture I would receive from Mama. She wasn't a policeman who said, "Wait till your father gets home!" nor was she the timid kind who would wail when she heard I skipped school. She would just very quietly and forcefully tell me, "If you don't go to school, you will be a dunce!"

After a while, Mama's brilliant tactic towards discipline drew a response from all of us children. It's easy to act like a child when your parents treat you like a child, hollering, slapping or throwing temper tantrums. It's harder to speak to a parent who treats you as a fellow adult asking quietly why you acted so stupidly. After a while, you have no choice but to act like an adult and say just as quietly, "Yes, that was stupid! I'll try to do better."

That is not to say that at times the solution might be a quick slap on the rump but rarely! And only as an attention-grabber. Reason is the only real answer to raising children- reason that teaches and explains why. It takes much longer and requires more effort, but it is certainly more lasting. To this day I get angry when I see parents slapping their children, or hurting them to force them to do things their way. But parenting is a tough job! I forever thank God that I was blessed with parents who had the good sense to discipline us with love and kindness, and not with anger.

> EDITOR'S NOTE: Amen, Pop! I still remember the lectures. A slap on the rump would have been shorter, but probably not as effective.

In the Italian tradition, Mother was also an ardent Catholic and faithful churchgoer, going to Mass just about every morning, while my father (just as ardent) was not so evidently spiritual. Men were expected to be religious, but attending Church- except for special occasions such as Christmas, Easter, marriages, and funerals- was just not something men did. Papa did, however, go more than most. We always went to very early Mass on Sunday before going to the fields or beginning whatever project we had planned for the day.

Though everyone in town was Catholic, many of them were anti-clerical. My father, with two uncles as priests, was both a target and a beacon for others. He was a respected man in the community as a successful businessman and warder of the Church, and extremely popular because of his even temperament. I believe, however, that his quiet faith must have been a source of inspiration for those who hated the Church for one reason or another. Papa always listened to everyone's opinions, never took sides, and tried to instill fairness and reasonableness into every problem. I thank God for his example of always seeking "the middle ground".

In any event, no matter how people felt about the Church, it remained a major unifying force in all our lives. Everyone in Modugno "belonged". We lived close to the land and close to each other. Whenever anyone saw a priest go by it, it was our custom to kneel and pray for the person the priest was visiting or to whom communion was being delivered. A visit from the priest usually meant a sick call, which were normally serious affairs. Odds were, you knew or were related to the sick person. All the people in town knew one another; it was wonderful to experience such a sense of warmth and inclusion.

All my earliest memories center on the closeness and strength of my family. In joy, sadness, tragedy, exuberance, or whatever, my family was there and involved. We laughed together, cried together, and lived together. Even today, over seventy years later, these memories of both joy and sorrow bring tears to my eyes.

"GROWING UP"

I started school in Italy at age 6, and began to learn English when I was much older. I picked up quite a bit because I had three uncles in Canada who used to send letters to my mother (their sister). I heard my mother often talk about Canada and how cold it was and how they had snow. I used to wonder how anyone could live in that part of the world with such cold temperatures.

As an educated woman, Mama was very interested in my schooling, grades, and whether or not I attended classes. As the daughter of a major local landowner, she had grown up in a family that prized education. The Trentadue family was landed gentry. That didn't mean they were wealthy. They were more like middle class famers who had enough land to earn a respectable living from working it. By today's standards it would be small, but substantial in Italy then, if not now. Mama's family owned about a hundred acres of vineyards and olive groves. Mother's uncle, as I said, was a priest; and her brother Michael was interested in theology- he later went to Canada where he studied to become a Methodist minister, much to the chagrin of his uncle and the rest of the family.

Schooling was important to mother, but not a priority in the life of early twentieth century Modugno. In the first decade of the century, school or even "book learning" just wasn't considered very important in an Italian farming community. Mama fought valiantly against this idea- albeit a losing battle- with good humor, cheer and a ready smile. What I didn't learn in school, though, I learned at home among the bustle of household chores. Some of my lessons included caring for the younger children, even changing diapers if necessary. While I was a perpetual truant in my early school days, there were times when I gladly left home to go to school or preferably, out with Papa.

School was the proverbial one room affair, made out of fieldstone. The schoolmaster was a

"Master Frederico", who seemed so tall and thin when I was a little boy, and so frail and sickly when I saw him years later. We used to joke about him, wondering how many stones he carried in his pockets to keep from blowing away with the wind. My brother Frank was the one who found nicknames for everyone, including Mr. Frederico whom he called "number 11" because of his long legs and thin frame Years later, whenever we played bingo and the number eleven came up, we'd all remember Signor Frederico. Indeed, if I was with relatives or friends from Modugno, the number "eleven" wouldn't be called but "the legs of Frederico". We all laughed, not in derision, but in the fond memory of a good man.

The inside of the school house was basically a big room with long benches where three or four students sat on each bench. Master Frederico sat at a high desk on a raised platform at the front. The front of the room also had a large slate (blackboard), and we all had little slates or writing tablets. Paper was expensive and wasn't used until later grades. The school system in Italy consisted of primary, secondary, and university levels. Naturally, there was no university in Modugno. People normally went to a seminary or larger university in Rome or Bologna. Most students, like me, finished primary school, but only a few went on to secondary school. Though Mama had completed such higher education, Papa had attended only grade school.

As the oldest son in a large family, I helped with the family chores as much as I could. Couple this with my dislike for structured learning, and it was obvious that formal school and I were not meant for each other. Until I was ten, I did not care for school except as a place to have fun, or somewhere to avoid- except for

English class. That was different. I was more interested in learning to read and write English than I was in learning about Italian history, culture, or science. I always liked languages and in later life picked up a smattering of quite a few- especially French, Polish, Ukrainian, and even some German.

EDITOR'S NOTE: I found this part of Pop's transcripts humorous, to say the least. All through my life Pop hammered at my brother and me to learn-learn- LEARN!!! He certainly knew how important education was. I can still remember him saying- "Go to school and learn or be a dunce like me, and sweat all your life". You were some dunce, Pop. Would that everyone were as "educated" as you. I always felt Pop was the embodiment of the philosophy that "Education is what is left when you forget everything you ever learned in school!"

Nevertheless, Master Frederico worked hard and didn't give up on his students. He knew how important learning was and would be for us, but it was a tough environment. He tried; but we didn't. We wondered if he would ever get the message. He wondered how we would ever learn anything if we never went to school. He was especially worried about two scallywags who played hookey repeatedly- my buddy, Mauro Romita, and I. We were great friends and loved to laugh and have fun. Too much fun, I suppose, because we both spent three years in Grade One.

At any rate, we soon grew to be the biggest in the class and thought we had it made because we could organize things to suit ourselves- until we found out our nicknames among the other children were "The Dunces". Up to that point, we had been running the games, were on all the school teams, and basically "starred" as athletes because we were the biggest. We were really more class clowns than bullies, but we were also protectors. Whenever bigger boys picked on our classmates, we fought for them. (To be honest, we welcomed the occasional fight and rough and tumble that most boys enjoy).

One of the games I remember playing as a child was "buttons". Like marbles, the idea was to shoot the buttons into a ring with two fingers. You get four or five boys, bet money on who'll get closet to the center of the ring, and whoever wins gets the money. This was one of the games that preoccupied Mauro and me in school. We made quite a bit of money, too!

Anyway, Mauro and I finally did knuckle down to work and managed to complete the three missed grades in one year by going to night school. After that, school really wasn't that much fun anymore, but we moved up the grade ladder faster and actually graduated sooner than usual.

In later years, Mauro and I joked about those days, reminding each other of our pranks and how we entertained others around us. On Columbus Day in 1953, in New York City, Mauro was the General Chairman of the Columbus Day Parade. We were both on the reviewing stand with a number of dignitaries, including the Mayor and the Governor. Mauro was the Chairman of the Castle Coal and Oil Company. I had just had my second book published and been elected to the Epicurean Circle of London as a Master Chef. And there we were, the truants- the incorrigible pair who repeated Grade One three times because Master Frederico was convinced we would never succeed at anything!

EDITOR'S NOTE: Mr. Romita and Pop were great friends as adults, too. They always laughed in a very special way whenever they spoke of their childhood. I think it was wonderful that two such unaffected fun-loving guys did so well. Maybe their attitude was the reason why!

Obviously, Mama never had a problem with school; she also had the added benefit of private tutors. Her family, at times, felt she had married beneath her since my father was a merchant with little education. However, I guess this spurred my father to strive even harder to prove himself to his in-laws. Life for my parents must have been difficult and full of hard work, although I don't remember a single word of complaint from either one. Both Mama and Papa had strong personalities, but they were a team, each taking a leading role in managing both family and business. My father mostly ran the wine business; my mother primarily kept the finances straight and directed the children.

Then again, they didn't have the problems of small business people today. There were no government forms and little regulation. If you took in more than you spent, you made a profit; otherwise you had a loss and eventually went out of business. There was no such thing as welfare for people or companies. We all worked or we didn't eat; my family either ran our business properly or we went out of business.

Today, corporate politics seem to be more important than sound management. The heads of some large corporations are people who sometimes know very little about the business they are running. These "professional managers" just move from company to company often with more interest in their own advancement than in the organization they are working for. They are hired because they are popular, good at selling themselves, or can say the right things to the right people in the right places. Competence can only come with experience and knowledge. Sound management can only come from competence. Business success can only come from caring about the business and its employees. My father knew every aspect of our business, and he taught me everything he knew. Where he left off, Mama stepped in.

Mama was the bookkeeper, accountant, paymaster, and chef for our family business. The early example she set as a master in the kitchen served as a beacon to me years later. Her insistence on quality and overall good taste were instilled in me as guidelines I carried with me all my life. Her idea of complete appeal required a balance with the eye, the nose, and the taste buds- food had to be attractive, aromatic, and tasty. These three elements had to be in sync or they could not achieve excellence. Mama was an artist in the kitchen, just as she was in everything she did. "Eye appeal", in particular, became important to me later in life as a Master Chef. I knew that taste and aroma could be guaranteed by using good food and good technique. Putting the dish together, however, called for color, balance, placement, and just plain artistry. Cooking a good meal is always a joy. Artistic composition always completed this joy. Needless to say, the diner, too, was always appreciative of the balanced artistry. So, thank you Mama!

Working with Papa, on the other hand, was different. He was a "man's man", so to speak. In the Italian culture of that time, a man was head of the family. He was always the leader, the decision-maker and a beacon of strength in troubled times. The father was head of the household, the dispenser of discipline. He was a demi-god, if not king. That was the culture and the stereotype, but not the reality. Men, then just as now, had their strengths and weaknesses. The weaker the man, the more he blustered and worked his will on those around him. The strong man- the true "man's man"- knew his place, knew his duty, knew his strengths and weaknesses, and acted with reason. The stronger the man, the more he worked in partnership with his wife, and acted as example rather than tyrant for his children. That's what made Papa a man's man. That has been my own personal goal all my life as well.

> EDITOR'S NOTE: Pop certainly was a man's man. I always recognized and appreciated his being my beacon and example, and hope to follow in his path.

For Papa, I picked grapes, squeezed olives, tended grape vines and olive trees, waited on tables and cleaned wine vats. Most of the time it was fun, but cleaning wine vats was a tough and sometimes dangerous job. The vats I cleaned were huge, as big as a large bedroom. These vats were built in place by the carpenters in Modugno. The older they were, the better the wine. They were made of wood and stored about 1000 gallons of wine. They were built with a neck and wine hole at the top. A trap-door entrance was located on the side of the vat towards the bottom. The top entrance holes were very small to keep air away from the wine. As a result, only young boys or small men could clean them. I always asked for the job because it gave me a feeling of helping, of being "big". Reluctantly, Papa agreed, but insisted I never go into the vat alone without our hired man at the vat opening to help me.

Normally, the vat cleaning procedure was safe. When it was emptied of wine, the trap-door was opened for a few days to let the fumes rise and allow fresh air into the vat. The cleaner was then lowered into the vat with a rope. The object was to scrape the walls down, removing the accumulated grape residue. To do this, I used a hammer, scraper, stool and small step ladder- but the most important thing was a candle. When it went out, the air was bad and you had to get out fast.

Once, for some reason, the vat didn't air out very well, and unknown to me it was full of fumes and carbon dioxide. Shortly after entering the vat, I became faint and very quickly slid down the rope to the bottom. I was stunned and hollered for help, but the boy who was working with me had left to do something else. I continued to yell, but he didn't come back. Then my candle went out; even worse, the side door was stuck. I started to kick the barrel and pound on the walls, feeling more and more faint. Just when everything seemed gray and white, and I was on the verge of passing out, I saw a light at the front side of the barrel. Then I heard the most beautiful sound in the world- my father's voice.

He told me to be brave and that help was coming. In a moment,, I felt a breath of air and saw a light. The helper was coming down the rope and my father was fanning fresh air in at the top. Between the two of them, they hauled me out. After that, I made sure our helper, Joe, was always near the vat when I went in, and that the door was fully open. Somehow, I think Papa always stood close by too, without telling me.

A few weeks after this incident, I had the opportunity to play hero myself. Every Sunday, I would clean my grandfather's stables with Mr. Sabino, a hired man my grandfather had do odd jobs. He had both chickens and horses, and Mr. Sabino and I would hose down the stable's concrete floors and sweep the manure and straw into bags. I would carry these bags to Mr. Sabino, who would in turn throw them over his shoulder into a six-foot deep drain near the highway. These drains functioned as septic tanks and were the size of a swimming hole. When it rained, they would get full of water that mixed with the manure and straw to form a mucky substance. This muck made a wonderful fertilizer- farmers didn't have to buy it back then. They just hauled out with a pail and used it on the fields.

On this particular Sunday, Mr. Sabino was tired. I was about twelve or thirteen, and standing on top of a wagon that was piled high with full bags. Usually, I would carry the bags to him one by one, and he would throw them over his shoulder and empty them into the pool. Anyway, Mr. Sabino happened to slip on one of the bags, plunging head first into the pool. All I could see were bubbles and his legs kicking. Quickly, I grabbed his collar, and managed to drag him out of the pool. His face and chest were covered with muck and he was gasping desperately for air. I quickly cleaned him up and then helped him to his home to get clean clothes.

We did finish emptying the manure bags that day, but afterward, Mr. Sabino told all my father's friends what I did. The talk of the town was that I had saved his life. Naturally, my family was very proud of me. I was just glad I had used my head instead of panicking. Still, deep down, I was especially happy that I had done something to make Papa proud of me.

"LIFE AND DEATH IN ITALY"

Papa and I were great pals. As the oldest son, I was privileged to have an especially close relationship with my father, and went everywhere with him. This wasn't so much our culture, but the normal situation where a father likes to spend time with his children- especially his sons- by showing them how and where it works. Sometimes this was fun, and sometimes it wasn't. One experience I remember vividly was seeing my sister's grave. Nicoletta had died shortly after my tenth birthday, from what must have been a severe strep or staph infection of the throat. Since it had been only a few weeks after her First Communion, my parents had buried her in her white communion dress.

It's tough learning about death when you are very young. Nicoletta was a constant companion for me and my brother, Frank. All of a sudden, she was gone forever. All of my family members grieved, but I think I may have grieved a little more because we were so close. I know now- though I didn't know it then- that losing a child is something a parent never truly gets over. Time heals the wound, but the scar is always there. As an adult, I can now understand why my father asked me to go with him to see my sister.

Land in Modugno was too important to be used for cemeteries, so each parish had a burial vault for its parishioners. In our parish, this was a large circular building with row after row of coffins. My father happened to be a "warder" in the parish, a job that entailed the supervising of the annual cleaning of broken caskets. One day before leaving the house for the cemetery, Papa approached me and asked if I wanted to see my sister. I was a little scared, but determined to go with him. Papa said he wanted me to come along because he felt I had to learn about life and death. Now, I also realize that Papa wanted to prepare me for the day when I, too, might have to view my own child's grave.

When we got there, the workmen were standing around wearing their handkerchiefs as masks. It was their way to say a short prayer for the dead before they began work, and as they prayed, Papa seemed quiet and humble as he led the men into the burial area. Then he came back to get me and led me inside with his arm on my shoulder- the stench was terrible as we went past the work area. Eventually, we came into a bright area with lots of light and flowers, and Papa led me over to a glass covered coffin. The sight of what was left of my little sister shocked me; decay had set in. For a moment, I was shocked and frightened. Then I started to cry. But my father hugged me and told me never to be afraid of death, that it was the common destiny for all of us. Then he repeated the Biblical saying that Catholics associate with Ash Wednesday: "Remember man that thou are dust; and unto dust thou shalt return". I hugged my father some more. We both cried. Then we left and went about the business of living.

I've always felt the Church is forever wise in its help in times of grief. Making people realize that we are all dust is not a harsh, senseless diatribe against living, but really a kind and paternal way of preparing us to face our own mortality. I have always looked upon the Church's message of "dust" as one of hope, as one of telling us to live in joy since life on earth is only a temporary existence. As I faced the death of others throughout my life, and even as I faced my own, I always felt a sense of comfort in knowing that I understood the mortal nature of life. I missed those I loved when they died- missed them more than I can ever truly describe, but I understood and I accepted, even if regretfully. I questioned God, and I questioned Him severely when my son died and when my first wife died so young, but I also accepted it. Otherwise, I truly believe such loss would have severely affected my mental health. But everyone is mortal. Seeing my sister's grave and her partially decomposed body at a young age drove home lessons that have helped me through life.

Afterwards, I better understood what death really was- not some mysterious or evil curse, but a part of the natural course of all living things. In Modugno, we were surrounded daily by life and death as we worked hard to wrest a living from the soil. No one had time for fakery; when someone died, they were dead. We did not spend large sums of money for a public show the way people do today. I feel the modern burial service is a sham in its attempt to make the dead look lifelike. I have been to wakes where the corpse looked better laid out than in life, and also marveled at the flowers for the dead, who themselves may have never spent a penny on flowers while alive. The hypocrisy of this is more sickening than that day in the churchyard. That was real, and I thank my father for trying so hard to teach me to live by showing me the face of death.

As I stated earlier, Mama was very religious. Since Father went to church so early in the morning, Mama always made me go with her when I wasn't going to the fields with Papa. Her religion was one of acceptance, expectation and kindness; a much more human philosophy than the sterile "faith", "hope", and "charity" terms that cloud our human acts. Mama always had a kind word for everyone. More importantly, her charity did not stop the minute she left church, as so often happens with many others.

I remember one especially poignant example of this. It was Christmas day, 1909. As we left church that morning, we heard the tinkling of the portable church bell. The priest walked by, proceeded by two altar boys, carrying Communion. This was his usual routine for going on a sick call. Mama and I knelt in the street and said a little prayer as the priest passed by. Then, with a sad voice and a tear in her eye, she said how terrible it must be to be sick on Christmas day and that she hoped whoever was sick would recover quickly. When we got home, Papa hugged Mama closely and said he had bad news. Grandmother Martino was dead. The priest had just left. The sick call we saw was for her; Mama had said her prayer for Papa's mother. After that, I rarely slept at home again. Until the day I left Italy, I usually stayed with my grandfather, Domenic. We had always been close because I was his first grandson, and now that he was a widower, we became even closer. He, Papa and I spent a lot of time together, even going to church together.

We lived life at a different pace back then. Many of the games we played were impromptu or make believe. Simple fun and simple pleasures were important. For instance, in the early 1900's, there were no jet trips to the south in the winter or to the shore in the summer. We lived five miles from the ocean and it was wonderful there in the summertime. A group of us boys would get together and walk the five miles to the beach. We'd take sandwiches or some sort of food and when we got there, went into the ocean and had a swim. No one ever brought any bathing suits- we were only boys. We would jump around in the water and have all sorts of fun, and then walk the five miles back to town. When we returned, everyone would go home for supper and then get together again afterward to play in the streets until it was time to go to bed. That was our life.

No one ever took a holiday for a week or two; you never heard of such a thing when I was a child. However, my family would on occasion rent a cottage near the ocean. Our family was big though, so we kept rotating who was at the cottage. Everyone had a turn. As a boy, naturally I always preferred going with my father and brothers. Often Mauro and I, together with some of our friends, would also go for a day. Life then, as now, was no different- we always had more fun with members of our family or friends than with strangers or alone. Of course, when my mother and father were there, I'd be with them. Whatever the arrangement, someone always looked after the family business. It was bad business to close for a week just to go relax at the cottage.

Simple, quiet, wonderful. The first decade of my life passed according to a different beat of the drum than today's frenzy. They were happy days for me, and probably the happiest for my parents. It was soon to change with the turmoil and financial reverses that came with the depression of 1911.

DOMENICO MARTINO

CHAPTER TWO

OFF TO AMERICA
"THE NEW WORLD BECKONS"

In1911, an amazing contraption arrived in Modugno. It was a mechanically powered vehicle that would run on its own without the help of a donkey or mule. They called it an automobile, and it caused a lot of commotion. All the farmers and townspeople gathered around it and stared in awe. Cars may be taken for granted today, but in 1911 Modugno this car was the eighth wonder of the world.

It looked like a carriage, but had no horse harnessed to it. Later, I would learn that it was called a horseless carriage. Of course, for an impressionable eleven-year-old, it was a fun thing. It was noisy, it smelled, belched smoke, backfired, and scared all the donkeys in town. But it moved much faster than a cart with a horse or donkey, and it moved on demand. The horseless carriage didn't stay long; it belonged to visitors who had come to see the town doctor. All of us boys wished we could ride in it like our friend Chiccio, the doctor's son. At school the next day, we crowded around him to ask what riding in it was like. He told us, very bravely, that it was "nothing". I still remember the pride in his voice as he told us how fast he had gone-forty kilometers an hour! Imagine!

The next time a car came to town it wasn't such a big thing. Soon the doctor had one, and then there were more and more. Mama and Papa even talked about the possibility of getting a car themselves when it looked like her family, the Trentadues, were probably going to get one. Papa thought for a long time before deciding he would buy a truck for his three cantinas the following year, provided business got better. But business never <u>did</u> get better...

Something else arrived in 1911. It, too, caused a lot of commotion, but no fond memories. It was the Depression and it hit hard. Many people throughout Italy were unemployed and very little money was in circulation. Our family was barely making ends meet in Modugno. Forced to sell wine for 34% below cost, my father was left with no choice but to close two of our three cantinas. Through no fault of Papa's, the family business almost went bankrupt. Later, I learned that the Depression hit all of Europe. For us, however, our town was our world. No one really understood how it happened, but suddenly there were no jobs, no market for our wine and olive oil, and workmen had no money to spend in the cantinas.

My family managed to keep one hired man- Mr. Sabino. My father kept Mr. Sabino around to do the chores and odd jobs that always needed doing. He and his wife, Rose, acted as foreman and woman for both our business and on our farm. If it was the season where Papa needed more help, they would hire for him. The Sabinos would know just what my father wanted and always took care of it in a thorough and dependable way. They were also on a salary all year round, so when

Papa started having money problems there was some concern that we would no longer be able to keep them. But somehow we did. All throughout the Depression, Papa continued to employ the Sabinos out of both necessity and pride, and certainly kindness. The Sabinos had nowhere to go and Papa did not turn his back on a friend or employee.

To give you an idea of how bad things were, we paid Mr. Sabino about sixty cents a day for both him and his wife. Out of that money, they had to keep their house, buy their food and clothe themselves-even though that was a relatively high standard of living at the time. In Canada, the average salary for labor was about ten dollars per week; in Modugno, Papa was selling wine for two cents a quart.

I didn't understand much at the time. Now, of course, I understand how people can be caught up in an economic whirlpool that they can't control. But even today, almost seventy years later, I remember the calm acceptance of my parents. They knew they could do nothing but try to cope day-to-day with the situation. It was a sad time for my father and it upset him greatly to lay off workers he had employed for years. While my mother handled the extra work in our remaining cantina, my father took over the additional duties in the vineyards. As the oldest son, naturally, I was obligated to help out as much as possible and worked side by side with Papa. We worked hard tending the crops, but we had fun. Work started shortly after dawn continuing until the late morning, when we would stop for lunch.

I look back and realize it was the little things that changed most. We had no extra cash to buy anything, so if we couldn't grow it, we didn't have it. Papa was always worrying about trying to make ends meet. His formula was belt tightening, harder work and longer hours. The entire family gladly pitched in because the only salvation lay with us; there was no one to help. We had no government support or other outside safety net. If you didn't work, or couldn't work, then you didn't eat. Then you had to depend on family and community support or you didn't eat. We took care of ourselves and our own. We didn't need or rely on faceless bureaucrats.

One day the seriousness of our financial situation really hit home. We went out to work the fields earlier than usual- Papa wanted to catch up on the harvest because he couldn't hire any help. My brother, Frank, and I went with him. It was a Saturday and school was out. We walked to the fields, and picked grapes until mid-morning when we stopped for breakfast. Normally, we had cheese, tomatoes, olives, olive oil for the tomatoes, and wine and water to drink. That morning, as Papa opened the basket, there was only bread and olive oil. I innocently asked him where the cheese was. To this day, I can recall the expressions on my father's face as they changed from abject sadness to a wide grin. With a smile and a laugh he broke off two pieces of bread: a large chunk with crust and a much smaller piece without crust. "Right here," he said. He ate first from the large chunk, and then took a very small nibble from the smaller piece. "Here's the cheese!" Frank and I caught on to his "game" immediately and joined him. We laughed as we made believe, eating the smaller softer pieces of bread between the larger chunks flavored with olive oil. That day we truly lived Depression. We also found out that humor could help us to survive it.

When we got home that day, laughing and talking about the cheese, Mama and my sisters couldn't understand why we ignored the lunch they had so carefully prepared as we continued our game of "cheese". When we told them what it was all about, they, too, joined in.

That summer of 1911 was long and hot. Everyone in the family chipped in to help Papa manage the work. All of us children grew up fast, gladly absorbing our new responsibility in a spirit of family love and unity. Relatives acted together as single family- aunts, uncles, grandparents, cousins- all working together to somehow survive the terrible times when <u>nothing</u> seemed to make a profit. We worked hard in the belief and hopeful expectation that our sweat would make things better.

To everyone's dismay, things got even worse. Italy went to war with Turkey during the Balkan War of 1911-1913 over some trivial issue. For the most part, the war was a remote issue for the people of Modugno except that the young men were no longer around. Papa told me how glad he was that I was only twelve because at seventeen I would have to serve in the Italian military. At the time, it didn't make much of an impression on me except to make me wonder if the war was connected with the tightened money situation. In my young mind I began equating war with hard times. Now, after all these years, I can see just how true that connection is. It often seems governments that cannot manage their problems look for scapegoats, who are readily found in foreign enemies. To this day, I am convinced that many wars are waged as cover-ups for poor government.

In fact, it is often said that flag waving is the last refuge of the scoundrel. The true patriot does his job quietly and has no need for bravado. The truly brave just do what has to be done, and this was especially true early in this century.

My memories remind me just how real life was in those days. We lived close to the earth and close to each other. Family ties were strong because we depended so much on one another. My younger brother Frank was born in 1904, and it was a new experience and a great joy for me to be his older brother. By 1913, he had started coming to the vineyards with Papa and I. Frank and I became especially close, as a result. Leaving him to go to America was one of the sadder parts of my departure. But I'm getting ahead of myself. Suffice to say that Frank and I were great buddies. I was big for my age, but Frank was bigger (while I stopped growing at sixteen, he kept on). Perhaps the fondest memories I have of Frank were the times we went swimming in the Adriatic. Frank could swim like a fish. He also had a tremendous sense of humor, finding fun in everything. Frank had been in on our cheese game, too, and had invented new cheese names according to the thickness of the piece of bread and its relative amount of crust. His favorite was "Formaggio Casa Martino de Farina Bianco alle Oilio de Olive Verte" or "White Flour Cheese from the Martino's flavored with green olive oil".

The turmoil caused by the Depression and the war got Papa to thinking. He corresponded frequently with his brothers-in-law in Canada- Joseph, Michael, and Ralph- all Mama's brothers who were living in Toronto. Uncle Joe had been particularly successful, having invested in vineyards in California. Everyone he talked to told him how well they were doing and all the kinds of incredible business opportunities that were available. So finally, Papa decided to go see for himself. He thought he might be able to extend the wine business to Canada- exporting wine there from Modugno, or perhaps even starting a vineyard right there in America.

Papa was a smart businessman and knew the wine industry well. He either grew his own grapes or purchased them wholesale from other growers. He would hire pickers to harvest the grapes and haul them by wagon to the processor to turn into wine. Once they pressed the grapes and squeezed all the juices out, the liquid would be transferred to the huge vats in the basement of our wine store. The keys to success in making wine are connected to knowing how much sugar to add (and when), how long to leave the wine in the vats, when to tap the vats, and when to bottle the wine- and Papa was expert in all these phases. It was a long process that is normally handed down from father to son. Had the times not gone sour, I probably would have been selected to learn the family winemaking business with Frank and our youngest brother, Nick.

Of course, Papa had the added business knowledge and retail experience from selling his wine, too. In Mama he had the perfect partner- both in marriage and in business- because she handled the restaurant end of the cantinas. Based on both of their experience, Papa thought the easiest thing to do was to open a small cantina or wine store in Canada that would eventually grow and prosper. His ultimate plan was to use this as a starting off point into wine making in America. Furthermore, in Canada, there was not yet a grape-growing industry in southern Ontario, and little or no native Canadian wine industry. Papa was encouraged even more by Uncle Joe, who told him about the beautiful sunny climate of California and the wine industry just getting off the ground in the Napa Valley where Uncle Joe had purchased vineyards.

Papa really didn't understand the geography, politics, or distances in America. To him- and everyone else in Modugno- it was all "America". Canada and the United States were all one. It wasn't until later when we arrived in Canada that both he and I fully comprehended the facts of two separate countries, the vast distances between them, and the tremendous risks connected with the pursuit of a new business in a new land.

Of course, my father eventually chose to try starting the business in Canada because we had relatives already there. Besides Mama's three brothers who were living in Toronto, we had relatives in New York, Buffalo and San Francisco. It was important to Papa to have family close by. He had already inquired about possible locations and availability of supplies in Canada, and how to transport the bottles, vats, and merchandise from Italy. When he was ready to follow up on these arrangements, Papa finally decided the next step should be a short trip to Toronto to investigate the area himself. After that, he would come back, sell what was needed to raise capital for his business venture, and then officially emigrate to America with his family. That was the plan. I coaxed him into taking me with him. It was supposed to be a short trip. I never thought I would stay there for the rest of my life.

War clouds were forming over Europe…but I didn't care. I was about to embark on the most important journey of my life. And I was with Papa. In

March of 1914, my father and I left town to go to Canada.

"CANADA"

Naturally, leaving home brought mixed emotions. Pop-Pop Martino was unusually upset to see us go. He hugged and hugged me saying, "Please don't go; you'll never come back; I'll never see you again". I didn't. He died before I returned in 1923. It was especially sad to leave Mama. All my life, I had never left her sight previous to this. As a grown man, I went back twice to visit her and saw her only once. On my second return trip to Modugno she was not alive. By then, the same was true for Papa, too. Both had died during the Second World War.

My father and I were very sad to be leaving our family, but at the same time, filled with the excitement of starting a great adventure. Besides, we told ourselves, we were only going to be gone a short time. We would be back in time for the summer harvest. Many of our friends and relatives from Modugno came to see us depart on the train. This was an exciting moment, for at that time, there were few Italian emigrants bound for America. Today, people tend to take such trips for granted- in 1914, it was quite a different story.

There was an energy and anticipation in the air at the railroad station. Papa and I had to fill out very important-looking forms. Modugno had no train or train station. We went to the country capital, Bari, five miles away. Waiting for the train to come was nerve wracking. When it finally arrived and we boarded to leave the Bari station, everyone was waving and shouting, "Goodbye and good luck!" It was a big event for the people of Modugno! Everyone worried when someone left town to travel to a foreign country. Besides it being unusual for anyone to leave in the first place, the spotty and sometimes inaccurate news the townspeople received from abroad- like the weather reports- wasn't always good. Fortunately, most news that arrived about job opportunities, food, and housing was usually positive, and <u>accurate</u>.

One of the things that made my departure a little more bearable was that my friends made such a special effort to wish me well on my trip. I knew I would miss them. They gave me several small, but special gifts as "going away" presents: expensive "Macedonia" brand cigarettes, a scarf, a sweater and a quite fashionable hat that I treasured. They kidded me that I was going to a nice, cold climate, so that was why they got me all the warm clothing.

To be honest, I was most impressed with the cigarettes they give me since we all smoked and Macedonians were the best around. I suppose we all thought it was the "smart" thing to do, just as the youth of today do. From the age of ten we sneaked smokes. All of my friends smoked regularly, but I usually didn't want to even though they teased me. Deep down I always thought smoking was dirty and that it smelled bad! However, as often happens with boys of my age, curiosity finally got the better of me. There was one instance when I was about ten or eleven when I decided to try smoking and also get drunk. First, I drank a lot of wine, but I didn't really enjoy drinking it. Drinking made my stomach sour and my head dizzy, so I stopped. I quickly decided drinking to get drunk was stupid and haven't changed my mind since. I do like a well-made drink or a good wine, but certainly have no desire to get sick or lose control of myself. Thank God I learned at a young age how pointless getting high can be. Maybe it was because I was surrounded by wine my whole life and it was never a "big deal" to me.

Smoking the cigar, on the other hand, was fun. I puffed the same way I saw my father and grandfather smoke theirs. I eventually got giddy and must have walked a little funny because Mrs. Sabino noticed there was something wrong with me. She made me stop smoking and helped me get over being dizzy by sitting in her kitchen until I felt better. I begged Mrs. Sabino not to tell Papa because I wasn't too sure of his reaction. Papa had never hit me, but I didn't know if smoking cigars would finally be the "straw that broke the camel's back". Parents' use of physical discipline was the standard punishment in the Italy of my youth. I was unusually lucky to have an understanding and forward thinking father who believed in instruction and example rather than slaps. But every man has a limit and I was sure I was about to experience Papa's. On my way home, for some reason, I decided to hide the partially smoked cigar in the fence post.

A few days later- and I can still remember Papa's creative approach- my father sat smoking his evening cigar after dinner and called me over. I sensed trouble, but sat quietly. Papa began with, "I had a dream that you smoked a cigar." I remained silent. He went on, "I even dreamed that you hid it in the fence post. So I went there and found a partially smoked cigar. I'm glad it was a dream, but I still cannot understand why I had that dream. Shall we go look in the fence post now?" I quaked in my shoes. Damn! Mrs. Sabino must have told him what I did. What was I going to do? I decided to throw myself at my father's mercy. I felt ashamed that I had deceived him. With tears in my eyes, I threw my arms around his neck and sobbed as I asked his forgiveness. He hugged me, and stroked my head. "Don't drink or smoke cigars! Your day will come, so take your time growing up. Enjoy your youth, it goes so quickly!"

Anyway, my father did find the cigar, showed it to me and said, "See, my dream was right." At that point, I believed that he actually saw my misbehavior in a dream. Later, I asked Mrs. Sabino if she had said anything to Papa. She allowed that she didn't think it was good for me to smoke cigars. What was nice about this incident was that Papa treated me with respect, even though he was obligated to discipline me. He simply said, "Now that I know the truth, don't do it again." Papa never hit me- or the rest of my brothers and sisters- because he had an understanding with all of us. If we acknowledged we were wrong and promised to never do the behavior in question again, we stuck to our word and that was enough. That was the understanding: that none of us lied to one another and we always kept our promises.

Today, I realize how fortunate I was that my parents didn't believe in corporal punishment. Our family "arrangement" was just another example of my being able to learn parenting from a very wise man. In my own experience as a father, I have tried to stress more of an "arrangement" with my two sons. This always meant discipline needed to be creative and sensible, based on reason and not on pain. This particular smoking episode also made me take note of the special partnership between Papa and Mama. He handled the boys regarding "man-to-man" things and

Mama took the same sensible approach to the girls' problems, especially when it came to dating and sex. Thank God I had boys, though, I wouldn't know how to raise girls- it's too complicated!

Anyway, the train took us to our ship, the Palermo, which departed from Naples. Papa and I were fortunate. We were not poverty stricken immigrants travelling steerage- or third-class. We had our own second class cabin, although we did share it with two other passengers. I have to admit, the food was gorgeous and the voyage was beautiful. On our side of the cabin, I had the upper bunk and Papa, the lower. There were some days when the sea could get kind of rough, though. On the first day, I couldn't get out of bed. The pillow seemed to be stuck to my head. Every time I raised it, my head would spin round. In a way, it was kind of funny. After that first day, I got over it and it didn't matter if the boat rolled or the water washed up on the front of the ship. I was up every day on deck. It didn't make any difference what the weather was like. I thought it was all so much fun- a great adventure. Papa thought so too, until the weather turned stormy after we left the Mediterranean and <u>his</u> head became stuck to the pillow!

By today's standards, the <u>Palermo</u> was a tramp steamer. It certainly wasn't sumptuous. Even first class was sort of dowdy. Steerage, however, was almost abominable. For those passengers, there were long cabins, almost barracks-like. They cooked their own food and ate family style. Steerage passengers had communal bathrooms of a very primitive nature. Second class passengers ate in the dining room. Our cabins were for four and each had a bathroom. Our food wasn't quite as good as First Class and we had no entertainment. Despite these drawbacks, the ship was safe, relatively new, and carried more lifeboats than needed. (We sailed almost two years after the <u>Titanic</u> sunk, so safety was a prime concern for everyone.) The ship's registry was Italian, which also gave us comfort because the crew was efficient, courageous, and took safety very seriously. In a disaster we were confident that the discipline of the crew would save us. They made us practice a lifeboat drill every three days and required all passengers to keep their life jackets close by no matter where they went on the ship.

I suppose that for most people- even those in first class- the trip wasn't all fun and games. In fact, after that first day I was the only one who never got seasick. I couldn't understand how slightly choppy water could make everyone so queasy that they were confined to their cabins all day. The ocean's temper wasn't strong enough, however, to keep a curious thirteen year old boy from venturing up on deck. I fought the ocean and elements and loved every minute of it. (Forty-three years later, in 1957, I sailed the Constitution through much calmer waters. This time, I was very seasick and then understood what my fellow passengers to America had experienced!)

Papa used to stay mostly in the cabin. He tried to cheer me up and I tried to cheer him up, and even though we wouldn't tell each other our feelings, we knew we were both sad. Despite these feelings, the times we spent on the ship were for the most part happy ones. Everyone on board brought a trunk filled with food, and we would gather together for meals. At night, there would be singing and dancing- not performed by some group in a fancy ballroom- but by the travelers themselves. Oh, the parties we used to have!

Again, I clambered all over the boat, no matter what the weather. One day, I had the scarf and hat on that my friends had given me because it <u>was</u> getting chilly as we neared North America. A big storm was brewing and a gust of wind blew the hat that meant so much to me right off my head into the sea. When my hat blew away into the ocean, I thought, "What'll I do! I've lost my hat! Should I jump over and get it? No, that's crazy. If you jump, you'll die." I looked at my hat drifting away and felt so sad and stupid. I thought, "You lose. You better be careful from now on, dummy, you're on your own. You can't make thoughtless mistakes like that. If you come out in a storm, you push your hat farther down so it stays on your head." Though I realized I wasn't accustomed to this kind of weather, I still felt a great guilt and sense of responsibility for losing that hat.

When I told Papa about losing my hat, he was philosophical. Instead of criticizing me, he congratulated me on how I handled the situation. "I bet you wanted to jump in after it," he observed. "I'm glad you didn't. You would have drowned without getting your hat." Once again, it was an opportunity for me to learn. Papa turned the incident into another lesson. I felt sheepish, stupid, and sorry. If only Papa had shouted or slapped me or vented anger, I would have been able to react in the same way to excuse my blunder, but his reason stripped me of this "cover". I'm sure my own sons felt this way when I used reason to strip away their excuses and covers.

After my lecture from Papa, I said to myself, "I've got to be observant from now on. More so than before." I also felt so frustrated that I went back to my bunk, grabbed the Macedonias, and had my first cigarette to comfort myself. I had never smoked cigarettes like these before; they were good, but kind of strong. As I puffed, I got dizzy. On the ship, you had to be careful because the ocean air is different and gets you dizzy faster. But being young, I was able to tolerate it. When you're young, you can stand a lot of punishment and fool yourself into thinking you can take it all, that you're super-human. Now, of course, I know differently, but you get all kinds of ideas when you're young.

That cold gust of wind was just an inkling of the weather I'd have to face in Canada. I wore the sweater a lot because I had no overcoat. In Italy, people don't own overcoats. We didn't want to come to Canada heavily loaded down with clothes and Papa just figured we'd buy what we needed. "They have stores," he said. I had to get one right away when Papa and I landed in America. My uncle was nice enough to buy me a spring coat. I thought to myself, "Coat, what's a coat?" At home, I had a suit and a light sweater, but that was it. It was <u>hot</u> in Italy! I thought I knew all about Canada, but didn't realize just how cold it was. Fortunately, Papa and I were prepared; we had enough money to cover our expenses.

As we neared America, we were given instructions by the Palermo's staff as to what to do, where to go and what papers we needed. All of us were issued sheets of cardboard that were to be attached around our necks with twine. Our papers had to be in order, in an envelope, and easily accessible. The cardboard "labels" had to list our names, port of origin, destination and intermediate major way points if we were going to travel through Boston to some other destination. Everyone also had a number. I had my father's number, with a "-1" to connect me to his number. Everything was written in English. I was relieved that I understood and felt sorry for those who did not. I could already see that not knowing English would cause problems for many of the passengers on board.

Papa and I arrived in Boston, Massachusetts on March 25th after departing from Naples on the 9th. We were actually allowed to enter Boston on the 27th after passing immigration early in the morning. Even though we happened to get through the immigration procedures quicker than most, it was kind of a peculiar time. Immigration officials used to pick and choose who could come into Canada. New arrivals had to be approved by a ship official, a doctor, immigration officials and a "guidance man". The guidance man was someone who spoke English and Italian and helped Italians get to the right place- he was supplied by the shipping line as a courtesy. This service was a major reason why Papa selected the <u>Palermo</u> for our crossing; he felt they cared. I felt the same way because I understood English and was able to realize how they truly protected and shepherded their "flock".

Though everyone was relatively kind to me because I was a child, the American Immigration Department in those days generally welcomed people as if they were high grade cattle. To make matters worse, we didn't even know if we would be allowed to stay, or if we would be "shipped" back. We tolerated all the indignities with patience, however. We were just happy to be here.

Unfortunately for us, immigration was strict about who came into the country- not like today, where it's more open. Humiliatingly, you had to take a bath for lice or any other "vermin" in preparation for the medical examination. But before you could even take this bath, all the men had to stand naked so the immigration officials could wash everyone all over first. That was part of the immigration laws! We were "washed" with fire hoses after we soaped down. Of course, I'm sure we provided a lot of fun for those who wielded the hoses. At least these indignities weren't suffered in vain. Incidents like these later led to the revision of the laws and processes for immigration, improving conditions for future arrivals. Papa and I were naturally incensed at all this, but we kept our cool. That was the price of admission. Our visitor visas were even ignored; we were lumped in with the landed immigrants because we hadn't travelled first class. Everyone was treated the same. What rot! I was so mad and embarrassed that I begged Papa to just go back on the ship. Once again, his patience and good sense prevailed even though I knew he was angry. In fact, I never saw my father as angry as he was then.

Having passed through United States immigration, and being released from Boston with the big cardboard numbers still pinned to our chests, our next step was to travel to Canada. Papa and I took a train from Boston to Toronto, arriving in Canada on March 28th. We passed Niagara Falls at the Black Rock and had another immigration check in order to get into Canada. They took our papers and because I could speak a bit of English I had fun chatting with the officials. We enjoyed our train trip by passing the time making jokes and kidding with one another. We had a few travelling companions with us from Boston and I remember one old man who caught my attention. He appeared to be reading an American paper, yet was holding it upside down. Bewildered, I approached him and asked why he was doing such a thing. The old man looked at me and smiled. "You're too young," he said. "You wouldn't understand. This is a language that can be read upside down." We both laughed and I told the man that he couldn't fool me. I had made my first friend in America.

Upon our arrival in Toronto, we were greeted by my uncles and several of their friends. They were thrilled to see us and glad that we had made the trip safely. Our Canadian family had a room prepared and all ready for us on Walton Street - that's near Yonge Street, the main North-South street in Toronto. Papa and I went to our new home in style by taking the modern, electrified Yonge Street streetcar. I had only ever seen horse drawn streetcars, but Toronto was apparently blessed with cheap electricity from Niagara Falls. All their streetcars were electric. It was a big, long polished wooden car with red velvet seats on both sides. There was one step to go up after the streetcar door closed and you paid for your ticket. Further up, the velvet-covered benches lined the inside walls- there were no individual seats in between like today. I wanted to know if it cost more to ride inside the cab of the streetcar; I had my eye on a soft velvet seat in the back. My uncles told me the fare was the same, no matter where I sat, so I took my place. The seat was just like the velvet chairs on the Palermo- luxurious and comfortable. I told everyone to come inside and sit with me, because it was so good. I remember even speaking in a low voice because it was so quiet and elegant in that streetcar.

It was cold when we arrived. There was a stove in the back of the streetcar that burned coal. The conductor had double duty. He collected tickets and tended the stove.

There was a smell of smoke in the car, but the heat radiated in a glow from the stove. If you wanted to be warm, you sat close to the stove. Since most people wore heavy overcoats, there was no need to sit too close to the heated sides of the stove, surrounded by a short metal fence enclosure to make sure you didn't fall over the stove and burn yourself.

Since we were wearing thin clothes, we sat close to the stove to keep warm.

Later on, I learned that even single man streetcars carried stoves. In these, you paid as you entered. The motorman-conductor stopped periodically to "crank" the stove.

Not all streetcars had the red plush seats of the Yonge Street line. Some of the older cars on other lines had all wooden seats. Toronto was blessed with cheap electric power from Niagara Falls some seventy miles away so the street railway was electrical even in those early days. Only some of the newer outlying areas had horse-drawn cars.

My first impression of Canada- or Toronto- was of elegance in the red plush seats, and the bitter cold. Even in late March the winds blew and the temperature was close to freezing. As I got older, I noticed how the winters seemed to be getting milder. A lot of scientists were predicting warmer winters for some odd reason or another. As far as I was concerned, the more people who live in a city, the hotter it gets from all the people, building heat, and pollution. The winters are milder now because there are a lot of people in Toronto. Maybe there are other factors, but that has to be a major reason.

The streetcar ride from the train station to our home was relatively short. It was dark when we finally arrived at Walton Street. There was snow all over and it was cold! All the way to Canada on the train, there had been snow everywhere, and I thought to myself, "By golly, it's the way they explained it to me. Look at the snow!" I got the biggest thrill from seeing all that snow. I'd only seen snow once before in Italy and it melted right away. But when I got to our room, and saw all this snow around me, the feeling of excitement and exhilaration left me and was replaced by a calm, peaceful feeling. At that time, people didn't have plows and they used shovels to clear the snow. There'd be piles of snow on corners and near the sidewalk. It was strange...I'll never forget the impact of all the new things I saw at the time. I felt glad I had come.

This was a wonderful and peaceful country so far as I could see (there were only 250,000 people living in Toronto the year I arrived). I was absorbing all the details in every shape and form for I'm not a person who doesn't notice things. My uncle lived on Walton Street and his landlady was from Modugno, so we didn't feel at all like strangers. Together with our relatives and friends, we had quite an enjoyable evening. Papa and I received a warm welcome and the landlady prepared a nice dinner for us. When we at last retired to our room, there was a comfortable, clean bed and nice things around, and so we settled in. "Well," I said, "This looks pretty good."

As I went to sleep that night, I dreamt of home, of mother, of my brothers and sisters. I was on a great adventure, but I missed them. As much as I was happy to be in America- or Canada- I was still a little homesick. I was only thirteen. All of a sudden, though,

I knew that my childhood was over. I was barely a teenager, without really knowing what that means in today's context, and I was in a man's world. As I said my prayers, and burrowed down into the pillow and my bed, I vowed to act like a man and to make Papa proud of me. Perhaps I even shed a tear for the "death" of my youth, but I can't remember. I do remember how tired I was.

Once again we were in the bosom of our family. Here we were, across the ocean from home, and we were met by my mother's oldest brother, Uncle Francesco, and by his younger brother, Uncle Raffaele. Uncle Joe was in California but due back in a few days. As I went to bed that night, I felt safe and secure, surrounded as I was by family. I didn't realize I was "home"- a new home in a new world.

I do love this part of the world dearly. I also love the land where I was born. I love America because my family is here, my wife and my sons. Naturally, they have their families here, too. My roots are here now. I never dreamed I would come to look upon Canada as my true home. While I was born in Italy, I came here before my fourteenth birthday. I came as a boy. I stayed to become a man, a father, and now an old man. It is such a beautiful country to live in. Thank God I came here!

CHAPTER THREE

LIFE IN A NEW COUNTRY
"ADJUSTING TO CHANGE"

I remember well the primitive Canadian lifestyles of 1914. The house on Walton Street had neither a furnace nor central heating; rather, there was a large pot-bellied stove in the center of the hall that burned coal. The bathroom facilities were outside the building- the "backhouse", as it was called. For me, using the backhouse was a nuisance. The smell was especially distasteful. We had been fortunate in Italy to have indoor plumbing. This was due to my father's industry and mother's fastidiousness. While Papa and I weren't used to these inconveniences- even more so in such cold weather- we learned to live with them. Eventually, we did move to a building with more modern facilities.

While we lived in an Italian household, the food was different than in Modugno. While Italian, it was "Canadianized". We ate more meat and potatoes, and less pasta and bread. I missed the wide variety of fresh vegetables of meals at home, but soon became accustomed to more meat. Native Italian diets are heavy in carbohydrates needed for energy. We were also used to eating our heaviest meal at a long relaxed lunch before we went back to work. Eating like this is now the accepted good health standard of today, and though we didn't know it, we really had quite a healthy diet in Italy.

Eating habits in Canada, on the other hand, were geared to a single long work day with the heaviest meal served at night. There was also a great deal more fat in the diet, and less carbohydrate and protein than in Italy. It helped us stay healthy, but put on weight! No matter how hard I worked, I soon lost the straight up and down lines I had in Italy and started getting pudgy. It wasn't until later in life when I returned to heavy carbohydrate meals and with my heaviest meal at lunchtime, that I lost weight and once again became "svelte". As I near eighty, I am approaching my weight as a teenager.

Canadian customs and attitudes are different, too. There seemed to be more of a brusqueness and businesslike atmosphere, which I assumed to be due to the greater industry and the cold. You don't dawdle when it's always so cold. As I grew older, I found that the further north or east in America you were, the faster people moved and talked. In the west and south, the pace of life was more relaxed; even speech became more of a gentlemanly drawl. Having come from the southern part of Italy, I suppose I was more of a "southerner" at heart. However, I soon changed. Within a year I was just as brusque and in a hurry as my fellow Torontonians.

Of course, for the first few weeks, I behaved like a tourist; there was so much to see and so many new experiences to tackle. Having come from a much warmer climate, I found Canada's climate particularly fascinating. In Italy, the waters were always warm enough for swimming. Here, I could walk across the water- the frozen Toronto Bay. In the summer time, because Toronto is on Lake Ontario, we went to the beaches. They were clean, but even then the water was always cold. At the warmest, the lake's temperature was in the low sixties. This was a far cry from the warm Adriatic I knew in Modugno!

Canada in the early 1900's was a primitive but extremely beautiful country. Its population was just beginning to expand and I was there to witness the growth. Toronto in 1914 was still considered a "big town" though. While progressive and modern, it did not yet have the high rise buildings of New York or Boston that I had seen on the train ride. However, compared to Modugno, it was gigantic and the buildings looked like skyscrapers to me. In my lifetime I have seen those buildings grow first to forty stories in the twenties and thirties to "towers" twice that size in the sixties and seventies. Then, wonder of wonders, the CN Tower went up in Toronto; it was the tallest free standing structure in the world. This little boy from Modugno was like a kid again when I went to the top of the tower last year. Having dinner and looking across Lake Ontario at my beloved Toronto as the restaurant rotated made me feel like a king. I felt privileged to have lived to see my adopted home come of age as the beautiful, powerful and dynamic city that Toronto is today- the envy of many other cities.

As newly arrived immigrants, we had little and expected little. We made our own fun, mainly by being together and enjoying each other's company. Whenever anyone else arrived from Italy, it was time for a party- we sat around, had a few cookies, drank coffee or beer, talked, told jokes and sang. If we were lucky enough to have someone who could play a flute or accordion, then it was a really great time! Sundays were especially pleasant times for family gatherings. We all pitched in, cooking together, sharing food and enjoying each other's company. When the weather was good, we went to the country for our picnics.

To get to the country, we would take the streetcar to the end of the line and walk the rest of the way- about a mile or so. For a change, we sometimes took a ferry boat ride to the Toronto Islands across the harbor. Toronto had an excellent streetcar system; though there were some automobiles, they were strictly for the wealthy. The old Yonge Street line streetcars had both a motorman <u>and</u> a conductor. Some of my father's friends worked on the streetcars, so we often exchanged pleasantries as we rode to work, to visit or to picnics. Going to the country was always fun. "The country" is a nostalgic phrase for me…this area is now within the city limits! Beautiful buildings, homes and high rises now stand where I played ball and socialized with my friends. Progress is important, but I do miss the rural openness.

When I was preparing to leave Italy, I suppose I built Canada up to be more than it really was to impress my friends. When you're young, your imagination can easily run away with you. After the first few days in Toronto, I realized it wasn't going to be as rosy as I thought. Papa found the language barrier difficult for him to deal with. At his age, it was hard to learn English as fluently as he wanted. For me, it wasn't quite so bad. I was young and could learn new languages with little trouble. But it was hard on my father- although, because he was a businessman with money, he did have the luxury of paying people to translate for him. (You "buy" brains when you can't learn!)

Maybe it's just the tricks our minds play on us, but my childhood memories of Toronto are full of nothing but the joy of a young boy on a new adventure. Just as I always remembered how grand the houses and streets of Modugno were, when I returned in 1957, I was surprised how narrow the streets had become and how small the houses actually were. Likewise, the memories of the smelly wood stoves in the streetcars and cold back houses are stored in the furthest recesses of my mind.

One thing I do remember from my Canadian childhood is how I was often looked down upon. Italians were not respected by the French or English because we were different. I guess it was the fact initially that we did not speak French or English that set us apart but, unfortunately, the prejudice continued even when we did speak good English. The stereotype of the Italian was someone who was short, dark, and spoke in a halting, pigeon English. I didn't fit the stereotype. I was fair-skinned and spoke English (and soon with little or no accent); I didn't encounter as much prejudice as some of my friends did. Unfortunately, this prejudice continued on until after World War II. Yes, prejudice was quiet; sometimes nothing more than a lifted eyebrow- quiet exclusions without any great significance. While it was annoying, it did become very serious business in the early days of the war when my brother Frank's store was broken into, destroyed because he was Italian, despite the fact that he had nephews in the Canadian Army. It didn't change the fact that we weren't totally accepted. This changed as the wave of immigrants from Europe and Italy came to Canada after the war. Instead of barriers being raised because they were different, they were accepted because of that difference. Toronto became very cosmopolitan because of a greater appreciation of the multi-cultural nature of different races. There are sections of Toronto that have their own special language and that is one of the things that gives this great city its charm. I am happy to say that today all prejudice towards me seems to be gone. Perhaps it's because I am an old man who is a respected member of the community. Though I no longer see prejudice against Italians, I often wonder about the new immigrants, from wherever they originate. I truly hope and pray they are able to feel welcome and do not have to experience the heart-wrenching pain of blind bigotry.

I suppose coming from a small farming community seriously beset with financial difficulty, the new world to me was indeed one with streets paved of gold- the gold of challenge, opportunity, and adventure. To this day, I am grateful that Papa took me with him to Canada. Was I luckier than the numerous other immigrants who came with nothing? Though Papa and I weren't destitute, we had only slim resources. We still had to watch every penny, and to complicate matters, being from an educated merchant family, we didn't have the luxury of taking any job that came along. While short of means, we felt we had to maintain our dignity. Because of our background, we were expected to do better and be better than the truly poor. Papa and I couldn't sulk, feel sorry for ourselves, or even hint at dissatisfaction- we had to be upbeat no matter how depressed we were, even though life was just as tough for us as all the other immigrants. There was no more a tangible class system in Italy than there is in France,

Germany, or England. The distinctions are really economic. Cultural pressure conceded with "maintaining appearances" were not so much class or cultural as individual pride. I think in the earlier part of this century, we had more of a feeling of self pride than we do now. Our way of life now is certainly much more free and easy. The rebellion of the 60's did much to eliminate some of the phoniness of distinctions between people. The youth of the 60's brought forth a sense of honesty that is refreshing; but on the other hand, other problems came up as well. It is too bad we cannot have the best of the 60's with the best of the 20's.

I suppose I feel that because of growing up with this family outlook, my life has been one of luck and charm. And yet I suffered through real tragedy. I grew up more or less on my own, was broke many times, and experienced terrible depression; yet I always kept my cool, and tried to look for life's good side. I have a naturally upbeat personality and believe this optimism kept me sane and alive throughout danger, sickness, personal tragedy, and death, as well as keeping me buoyant at fourteen when I felt like crying.

EDITOR'S NOTE: Pop's upbeat nature is not a contradiction to his suffering. He was a very sensitive man. I was there the night my mother died and saw how it almost tore my father apart. But he also knew he had to protect us. Falling apart and taking comfort from his sorrow would not help him or us. Hence, his basic upbeat and optimistic nature took hold. I am sure he grieved privately many times. Even on the tapes he dictated for this book, he skirted the issue of private sorrow. But I saw it and know it was there! Pop grew up in the mold that "men don't cry"- or at least not in public, or on tape. Despite his humor, he truly suffered growing up. Pop always felt he was fortunate- that he was "lucky"". Compared to thousands of other immigrants, it would appear that he had it easy- but he really didn't. I have always thought Pop's upbeat attitude was remarkable…not remarkable so much because of specific tragedies- everyone has to deal with tragedy. It's remarkable because so many people didn't have this attitude! No matter what their age or life experience (good or bad) most people never appreciate life and its small blessings. Pop's uniqueness lay in his ability to handle (and appreciate) anything that life threw at him…whether it was adventure or loss, good fortune or bad, he was always able to put things in perspective and find peace. The love and support he received from his family, along with a very good self-image, sense of self-esteem, and his belief in God gave him his wonderful coping skills. It proves that an upbeat approach can conquer terrible loss. Later, Pop's losing two wives and a young child certainly was not "lucky"- that's life at its most basic level. Pop coped!

Once Papa and I solved our housing, food, and clothing problems, we were able to settle in and get down to business. My father thought that school was the best thing to keep me occupied while he looked into opening a wine outlet. I didn't really want to go to school at all, but suggested to Papa my going to night school so I could work during the day. I didn't know what I wanted to work at, but was ambitious and very observant. I was also physically big, so I thought I was a man ready for the world and was determined to prove it. I started going to night school. Unfortunately, because of my inexperience with the language, I had to start school again in first grade. Unlike my early school days, I didn't play truant- this time I wanted to learn. I quickly mastered not only English, but also the history and geography of Canada. Being young gave me many advantages- the most important one being that I was able to learn English easily. This would be a critical factor for my success in both school and work.

After having been in Canada for only four months, Papa decided it was time for him to return home. War in Europe seemed imminent. He was worried about Mama being alone. He had also received a letter that my brother, Nicholas, was ill. With the long time span between news in those days, he decided to stick to his original plan and return in time for the harvest. Permanent immigration to Canada would have meant more time away from his family than he wanted to spend during those troubled times. Also, the economic situation in Italy was starting to look brighter; bright enough to lure him back.

Naturally, Papa wanted me to go back with him. I was the oldest son and expected to take over the family business. But I didn't really like the wine business. I had also begun to get attached to Canada- I loved the beautiful country and was speaking English all the time. More importantly, I was past fourteen and if the war lasted four or five years, I'd be in the Italian Army. I didn't want to be forced into the Army for anything! I had no interest in killing people or having them try to kill me. I'm not a violent person and don't believe in using force to solve any problem!

So my father rethought the situation and decided that he'd go back to Modugno and I could return later depending on the progress of the war. He reluctantly agreed to leave me with my uncles and promised to send money for the voyage back to Italy whenever the time came. Papa actually wound up sailing back to Modugno on the last passenger ship to leave New York. World War I started shortly afterwards, with Italy joining the Allies the following year. Mama's two brothers, Uncle Joe and Uncle Ralph, went with him. Uncle Mike, however, stayed in Toronto. I was left in his care and that of my other relatives and "paesane" (fellow townspeople) who were in Toronto. Paesane always acted like kinfolk. It gave all the Italian immigrants an extended family. Whether related by blood or by neighborhood, extended family always pulled together and helped one another. While alone, I had a lot of people watching over me.

To be honest, though being on my own at fourteen was an adventure, it was lonely. I was used to being surrounded by the love of many family members every day of my life. Many nights I felt very sad and depressed. I cried at times. In those days there was no radio or television to distract you. What distractions there were came through visiting, meeting with friends, meals together and basic human fellowship. At that time in my life, human relationships, especially family relationships, were vital.

This was especially true in 1914 after my father left. But as time went on, supported by the family that I had in Toronto, my depression eased. In my case I also found hard work was a convenient way to forget about my problems. I not only worked long hours, but continued going to night school to improve my ability to write and learn about the literature and culture of the English-speaking world, especially that of Canada. I also wanted to find out more about the political division within America that created Canada and the United States.

EDITOR'S NOTE: Hard work and schooling- formal or informal- were major coping strategies for Pop. This section where he mentions tears is rare in all the tapes he made in the almost five years he spent making them.

Besides, the exuberance of youth works wonders. My overriding motivation was to "make good", make a lot of money, and send it home to help my mother and family. I felt doing this was not a burden, but a privilege. I am happy to say that for the rest of my life I kept to this family tradition. I helped finance the emigration of all my brothers and sisters who wanted to come to Canada. It was a joy for me to be able to do this, and the memories of working for my family's benefit are happy ones.

EDITOR'S NOTE: Achievement was definitely another of Pop's coping strategies...that and working towards the betterment of the family.

After that first summer, I felt I had learned English enough to get by, and just as in Italy, I no longer saw any reason to go to school to "learn". By reading on my own I knew I could learn faster than in school, so I dropped out in order to enter the business world. At that time, not many people felt it was important to attend school, and those that did looked for an excuse not to continue. For me, work was more important.

EDITOR'S NOTE: Our family has always had an independent streak. Hence, Martinos usually choose to be businessmen, craftsmen, or professionals. It has never been a case of work being too menial so much as the desire for being your "own man". Some readers might consider shoe shining and being a chef menial. But you can take pride in any sort of work if you do your best, excel and move on! Martino family members have always sought independence, self-reliance and self-improvement. It's our family tradition of being free, self-employed, and willing to trade risk for freedom. The family tradition for Pop, then, was to succeed and get ahead.

Someone came along one day and suggested I shine shoes. This came at a time when I was selling newspapers and not making very much. I didn't understand what he was talking about, but he said I could make big money: $15 or $16 a week, maybe $20 on holidays. I had never heard of such big money. I asked him to explain what this business was all about. "Well," he said, "the black ones you shine for a nickel, and for the tan and red ones, you get a dime." In those days, men often had their shoes shined every day! Today, shoe shining seems like such a menial task, but in 1914, shoe stands were elegant affairs- plush seats on a raised platform made out of carved and polished wood. These stands were meeting places where the business of the day was discussed amongst the men as they read their newspapers and had their shoes shined. It was more a ritual than a necessity...the thing to do.

I found out that the best shoe stands were in barbershops, offering shoe shine boys a means of advancement to barber school and barbering. So, before Papa returned to Italy, I talked him into investing forty dollars for the stand and equipment so I could set up in the Palace Barbershop. Anyway, this same man offered to teach me and work with me for a week showing me what to do. We'd both shine shoes while customers were having their hair cut in the barber chair. There were five barbers at the Palace- it was a very classy place. A shave was ten cents; haircut, fifteen; shave and cut, twenty-five cents; and shoe shine either five or ten cents. I worked at shoe shining for about 5 or 6 months. It was a start, but only a start. The alternative was to sell newspapers, but that didn't pay as much. Eventually, I decided I didn't want to shine shoes or work as a barber. This wasn't what I had come to Canada for.

One bit of good fortune that resulted from my shoe shining business was that I got to know the head chef at the King Edward Hotel. He used to come to the barbershop and have his hair done by one special barber. He would also get his shoes shined and chat with me. We became friends, though I was only a boy at the time. One day I started speaking Italian and he asked me where I was from and why I was doing this kind of work. I told him I wasn't particularly happy shining shoes, but was just beginning to make my way in the business world. He suggested that perhaps I would like to become a chef like him. I often wonder why the idea had never dawned on me before as I always loved working in my family's restaurant in Italy. My chef friend pointed out to me, however, that such a job would not come easily. It would take a long time to work my way up the ladder; I would have to start out washing dishes, work up to a busboy, and then become a short order cook before I could move on to being a full-fledged chef. But he also said I'd never go hungry doing this kind of work. I knew it wouldn't be easy, but I was determined to give it my all.

"TEENAGE ADVENTURES"

I eventually sold the shoe shining business for sixty dollars and set out to pursue my new career as a chef. I had made my first profit in the new world! I immediately got a job in the restaurant business washing dishes at a coffee shop on the corner of Queen and Yonge. They used to call it "Queen's Lunch". I stayed there for six or seven months and, boy, that was hard work! There were two big sinks- one sink had the silverware and the other one cups- thick cups with coffee in them. In those days, there weren't many places to eat in Toronto. Queen's Lunch was fairly big; it even had two entrances. The kitchen was in the basement with all the short order cooking done on the first floor. I made sure I was fast with the dishes, so they let me help the cooks gather ingredients in the kitchen and get things from the storeroom as well.

Like I said, Toronto wasn't a big city then. In all of Canada, there were only nine million people. There weren't many people eating out either. But during the noon hour, a lot of customers would come in, even though they wouldn't eat much for lunch. They'd just buy coffee and a rice pudding, egg sandwich, or maybe pie- just a quick, light lunch. Sometimes, I'd hear the short order cooks taking orders for something like "stack of wheat". That meant wheat pancakes. The cooks had all kinds of phrases they used that were only understandable to those who worked there. Naturally, I'm now a Master Chef of Canada and have done everything from teaching to writing about cooking, so it's very simple for me to talk this language now. But years ago when I was just beginning, I thought it was all so very complex!

Sometimes, the regular cooks and other kitchen workers (sometimes even the waiters) would tell me to bring the "white" soup and the "red" soup to the kitchen. Anyway, white soup was chicken with rice and red was vegetable. So one day I said, "What do you want, the chicken with rice or the vegetable with barely?" They were impressed that I knew the difference. After that, I made sure I learned all the names of everything on the menu so I could find anything they asked for. I knew their kitchen inside out. It got so by the time I was fifteen, I was well known and had a good reputation with the restaurant staff. Eventually, they allowed me to fry eggs at lunchtime. I fried eggs constantly. It was all short order. I even worked up to frying bacon and sausage. So my initiative paid off. Before noon I was still a dishwasher, but at lunchtime I graduated to short order cook. Years later, I often remembered being given this important opportunity and always had a great deal of patience with young apprentice cooks and chefs. So long as they had energy and dedication and really wanted to learn, I made sure I had the time to help them.

After working at Queen's Lunch, I left to go to Child's Restaurant at the corner of Richmond and Yonge. It was a large establishment, one of the biggest in Toronto. Child's was known for its wheat pancakes and special muffins. I got a job working in the kitchen helping the short order cooks. (I guess I had more nerves than brains at the time- I was fifteen!) I told the owners what I had done and what I could do, and explained my experience and training from Queen's Lunch. They took a chance and hired me, putting me in charge of stock, too. I got to know the fellow who made their wheatcakes and muffins and he impressed me. He used to dress in white gloves. He was a thin man, nice looking and fast. I was assigned to help him and after I had been there for six months, he quit. Luckily, I got his job.

The wheatcake grill was in public view at all times but they had to be made in such great abundance and so quickly that I didn't have time to worry about spectators. Plus, if I didn't get the wheatcakes made in time, I'd get fired. I had to keep my mind on my work!

Consciously or not, I performed before quite large audiences at times. The job was fun, interesting, and more importantly, it taught me to be efficient.

When it comes to restaurant and hotel cooking, the chef who is the "chief" or "master" decides on the menus, specials, and amounts of the various dishes to be prepared. Depending on the size of the establishment, there are often numerous separate chefs in charge of different departments: a pastry chef, a roasts chef, a soup chef, a sauces chef, etc. The responsibility of these chefs is to prepare their foods or parts of the meal in advance- the roasts, the vegetables, desserts, etc. The serving chefs are the ones who prepare the dishes to be served as orders come in. Short order cooks prepare sandwiches, salads, omelets, or any items that can be made "in short order" (a short time). So, being a short order cook is the first step up the cooking ladder from pot cleaner, vegetable preparer, or steam table filler (someone who keeps replenishing the supply food where the serving chefs prepare their dishes).

Of course, a major factor in all cooking is cleanliness. Good food must be fresh, well cooked, tasty, and served in a pleasing dish. The appeal must be to sight, aroma, and taste. (Sometimes even sound is important, like the sizzle of a steak on a warm skillet. Therefore, it was important for me at Child's to have my work place free of crumbs or other debris that accumulated as part of the serving process. In order to make the wheat-cakes, I had a silver jug with pancake batter in my hand on the right, and on the left, I had a silver scraper jug with a special cloth attached to the front. This cloth was able to absorb all the crumbs from previous cooking on the grill. You had only a few seconds to clean it. I would take the batter jug with one hand and pour out all the pancakes in rows on the grill- up to a dozen at a time. Then I'd do the same with another jug. Of course, I had a special spatula to turn the pancakes; it was important to make them all the same size so they would turn properly. Then, the fun began. After all the cakes were turned, I had to flip them up in the air so they would land on plates that were resting on my arm and hands. You had to do it fast without missing. That was some job!

While I was working at Child's, I spent much of what little free time I had with my Uncle Michael. Papa had entrusted me to his care before he left for Italy, but because Uncle Michael was busy studying to be a Methodist minister, I was essentially on my own.

He and I were still living at the boarding house on Walton. I didn't see my uncle as frequently as I would have liked, although it was a comfort to know that he was always there if I had a problem. We shared a room together: he was always studying, and I was working seven days a week from twelve to fifteen hours a day. For a while, I was also going to night school when I could get there on time for classes. Life was certainly "full".

Even with so much to occupy us, we became quite close. I spent my first Christmas in Canada with Uncle Michael, and was there for him to help celebrate his ordination to the Ministry. We were great friends, later writing to each other often after he took up his ministry work in North Bay, Ontario, some one hundred or so miles north of Toronto. That Christmas of 1914 was a lonely one for both of us. As a junior helper, I had to work Christmas day in the restaurant, but I got home early enough to have dinner with my uncle and all the paesane at the Walton Street boarding house. Then on Epiphany (or January 6th- the proverbial twelfth night), Uncle Michael and I were finally able to exchange gifts. He gave me a scarf, as I recall. I think I gave him a shirt. Needless to say, on my first Christmas alone, I missed my parents and brothers and sisters terribly. I again resolved to save all I could to bring my family to Canada to be with me as soon as possible.

In the spring of 1915, I traveled to Depot Harbor, Ontario, hoping to take on the new job of assistant to the chef at the Depot Harbor Hotel. I had read an advertisement for this job in a Toronto magazine offering thirty-five dollars a month plus room and board and free transportation to Depot harbor, two hundred and sixty miles away. This job had a lot of appeal to me for two reasons. First of all, I wanted to break away from living in a "little Italy". No matter how much I wanted and needed the comfort of a family atmosphere, I also wanted to truly become a Canadian. In order to do this, it meant I had to break away from Toronto. My choice, finally, was to move to a small town where I could live as a young Canadian. Depot Harbor appeared to fit the bill. Of course, my second purpose in seeking the job was to further my career in becoming a chef. I knew that staying in Toronto would mean actively competing with a lot of other young men who were looking for kitchen work. By moving to a smaller town I hoped to bypass much of this competition.

I inquired about the job I saw advertised, but instead was offered the position of porter, which I gladly accepted because of the opportunity it represented. I would actually be employed by a Canadian news company that ran the different hotels and catered to the needs of the passengers of the old Grand Trunk Railway (now the Canadian National Railway). The news company operated all kinds of restaurants too, so when the train stopped, passengers could get meals and refreshments. At the time, the Grand Trunk had branches all over the line and kept both newsboys on the trains and boys who acted as porters to take passengers' luggage off the train for them.

In Depot Harbor, there was the hotel for the railway as well as a shipyard. Ships used to dock from all over the United States and bring their merchandise. It was a small town with a large transient tourist population. One of the main forms of entertainment in the days before radio, television, and movies was to go down to the train station each night at eight when the train pulled in. On Sundays when I wasn't working, I would sometimes go to the band concert in the park. The park also happened to remind me a great deal of the piazza in Modugno. To some extent, Depot Harbor was a sister city of Modugno- I guess that's why I liked it so much. I'm sure the good Lord also had a hand in directing my steps there, as it was a good substitute home in which I could grow to manhood.

As I said, Depot Harbor had a small normal population that exploded in the summertime. One of the main reasons was that there were more people working in the shipyard during the summer. At full capacity, there might be as many as 200 people and the hotel would be very busy. Naturally, in the summer the hotel brought in an expert chef for their busy season. Though we were open all year around, the shipyard would only employ about ten or fifteen people in the wintertime. I was young and not much of a chef, so the hotel used me during the winter when they couldn't afford anything better. I didn't make much money during the winter- the manager's wife did all the supervision and baked the cakes, pies and larger items herself. At least I had my foot in the door.

I stayed in Depot Harbor for slightly more than four years. I spent the bulk of my teenage years there, throughout the remainder of World War I and into the peace that followed. It was a wonderful town in which I would come to know many people. I felt at home there, as my friends created the warm family atmosphere that would always be so important to me. In the absence of my family, I found that good friends could often be more than a substitute. That is the small miracle I discovered in Depot Harbor, where I grew from youth to manhood, and from porter to a reasonably good cook.

The first time I went ice skating was in Depot Harbor. The manager and his wife had a daughter named Elizabeth. She and a girlfriend used to go skating all the time and always wanted me to go with them. They were just a year or so younger than me- but I usually didn't bother with girls. I grew up in a culture that reserved the start of dating for the late teens and early twenties. In Italy, people really didn't start dating until they were seriously looking for a husband or wife. However, I was gradually acquiring Canadian culture, a culture that allowed for having fun with the opposite sex without heavy involvement. So I started dating. In Depot Harbor, however, dating usually took the form of wholesome outdoor activities like hiking, canoeing, and of course, cross-country skiing- we had no mountains for downhill skiing, ice skating and ice boat racing. (I never tried ice boat sailing, but was often tempted because it always looked so thrilling and fun to hurl along the ice at great speeds on just an open sled with runners and a sail).

Anyway, about my experience with ice skating, I'll tell you...those girls were after me! Finally I gave in and agreed to go, so I bought myself a pair of skates. The rink was between the hotel and a church; it was beautiful, and Depot Harbor being a small town, there were a lot of kids there who knew me. Elizabeth and her friend took my arms and led me out onto the rink. We skated round and round and every time we turned a corner, I said, "Girls, watch that I don't fall. I nearly tumble every time." Although I was having fun, I kept having trouble turning at one corner in particular. All of a sudden, bingo, I was down. I got up and that was my first fall. The girls started to tease me and let me go and I fell again. I fell four or five times, more or less in the same spot. Despite falling, I was really enjoying myself and wanted to try skating alone. I even accused the girls of trying to make me fall. "No," they insisted, "we tried to help you. We want you to be a good skater so you can come with us all the time." So I tried to go around alone, but it was worse. I hit the fence. I walked around like a drunk. I couldn't stand up. I told them I couldn't go on- I couldn't even walk. They tried to talk me into continuing, but by that time, it was late and the rink was closing anyway.

I went back to the rink alone a few times trying to improve my skills so I wouldn't be so embarrassed to go with the girls again. But skating and I just seemed to be incompatible. Finally I quit going alone, and never went with the girls again no matter how much they coaxed me. I never mastered the beautiful and graceful art of skating. Looking back, I realized I had been wrong; I shouldn't have given up; I should have persevered until I could skate.

What I did enjoy during my free time in Depot Harbor was riding my bicycle. Needless to say, I didn't have much money, so I had to buy a secondhand lady's bicycle! I didn't understand the difference between that and a man's bicycle because I had never owned a bike in my life. There were bicycles in Italy, but I had always just walked around with the boys. At this point in my life, I was working in the hotel's restaurant as a chef for twelve hours every day and needed something to do in my off time.

EDITOR'S NOTE: Twelve hour days seven days a week were standard hours in resort areas then as now. Such hours were also common in the early part of this century in the restaurant business. It wasn't until the forties that a maximum forty-eight hour week was initiated, and later dropped to forty. However, even today, the hours in resorts can be long because of the "split shift" nature of having to cope with three meals over the entire day. It was normal to have a long break after lunch and before dinner. But even then, the total working hour-day was twelve hours, which was sometimes spread over a fourteen or fifteen hour time span.

After work I was often in need of some fresh air after my long day in a hot kitchen. So at night, I would take my bike and ride all over the downtown area. I'd get good and tired, and was able to sleep well so I could go to work the next day. I'd ride for two or three hours every night- but there were no brakes on this bike. Every time I wanted to stop, I would try putting my foot on top of the front wheel. It seemed to slow the bike down a bit, but wasn't really the kind of system you'd want to have in an emergency.

Once, I was riding fast right on Bay Street, at Richmond and Yonge. I was heading south towards a passing streetcar. It stopped suddenly and I realized I couldn't stop the bike! Ladies were getting off. I closed my eyes and was afraid to look. I thought for sure I would smash the bike or hurt people. Somehow, I wiggled through the crowd and people started hollering at me. I felt frightened and even more embarrassed because I knew I was supposed to stop. Another time, as I was accelerating around a corner, I came face to face with a speeding car. Just in the nick of time, I managed to swerve and avoid a collision. Unfortunately, I crashed into the sidewalk, demolishing my bicycle. Needless to say, this marked the end of my bike riding days.

Walking in the woods was another enjoyable pastime for me. Friends and I often hiked along the railroad tracks. This was always great fun in the summer, but somewhat dangerous in the winter. I always liked to walk and walking was certainly better in the summer than in the winter. While there was great exhilaration in this, there was also some danger. The woods surrounding the town were full of game-deer, bears, and moose. There were also birds of all kinds-and bugs! In the days before bug sprays, we tried home-made traditional kinds of "bug-off", but none really worked. I always hated bugs, especially the little gnats and black flies. When they got in my hair, I always felt like I wanted to wash my hair. Sometimes when the bugs were bad, I would look for the nearest pond and just jump in.

I spent Christmas of 1915 and '16 in Depot Harbor. In 1917, I decided to take some time off to spend Christmas with my Uncle Michael and his family back in North Bay. I had not seen him sine I was last in Toronto. In 1917, of course, Canada was in the midst of World War I and though only seventeen, I was big for my age- a fact that got me in quite a bit of trouble.

There was conscription in Canada during the first war. I didn't pay much attention to it because it took effect when a young man turned 18, and I was not only underage, but an Italian citizen. (I was not permitted to become a Canadian citizen until I was 21). Conscription, or "the draft", was rather unpopular outside Toronto. Many refused to serve or deserted the training camps. As a result, it became standard practice for the police to search trains for draft-evaders or deserters.

EDITOR'S NOTE: Feelings in Canada ran very high about conscription in both wars. In World War II, Canada had almost 9% of its population in uniform- a million out of a population of eleven million- and all volunteer. The government pledged that it would not institute a forced draft. When one was invoked in 1944, it was for non-combat duty only. Feelings were bitter on both sides. Those drafted blamed the government for breaking its word and those who volunteered derided draftees as "scabs" because they refused to serve in anything other than service groups- driving, stocking supplies, etc.

Several stops before reaching North Bay, two plainclothes government officials boarded the train. They went through each compartment asking questions of all the young men aboard. One approached me asking my name, where I came from, and if I was a Canadian citizen. Since my answer to the last question was no, he asked to see my papers. I was supposed to carry these with me at all times, but had honestly not even thought to bring them on this trip. I told him the truth, along with the promise that my uncle would be at the North Bay station to verify it.

Though Uncle Michael had been there earlier to meet me, the train was one and a half hours late and he had left temporarily. When I arrived at North Bay, there were two soldiers waiting for me. They took me to jail along with all the packages of food I had for Christmas dinner. I couldn't believe anyone would think a draft dodger would bring a big basket of fruit and a ten pound turkey with him! At any rate, my uncle arrived at the train station ten minutes later with his nephew nowhere to be found. Now I can laugh at this, but then I was one very frightened man! I was thrown in a jail cell with many other boys around my age. However, I must have looked more distressed than the rest because an officer singled me out and asked my age. I told him I was only seventeen and didn't understand why I was here. He asked if I had any money I could use as bail; I had fifty dollars and he took twenty-five. I might have been a lot poorer, but at least I was out of there.

By this time, it was 11:00 at night and I had to walk to my uncle's house. When I finally arrived, I opened the door and saw many worried faces. No one had known what to think when Uncle Michael wasn't able to find me at the train station. I explained what had happened and then everyone laughed with relief. The next morning, Uncle phoned someone at Police Headquarters, who straightened out the situation. Within twenty-four hours, I had my money back along with an apology from the officer who had arrested me. Though everything worked out for the best, it was at times like these I wished I had more of a baby face!

1918 was not a good year for reasons other than the war. I was still working in Depot Harbor, and had advanced from assistant to chef. The owners, the Rancias, treated me like a son- they were my "adopted" parents in this new land. Their son, Bill, was both a friend and a little brother to me; we spent many great times together.

I remember one incident in particular. Bill and I often went for hikes in the woods and frequently visited the local Indian reservation to see our friend, "Indian Joe". Indian Joe was an independent trapper, who had a tepee close to the river and the railroad. One Saturday in January, I took the day off to keep a promise to have dinner with Indian Joe. The weather was a little gray when Billy and I set out, but we weren't worried. Back then, there weren't any weather forecasts on the radio, nor was the information in the newspapers too accurate. We went by experience, by guess and by God...so there might be a little snow, so what!

Anyway, we set out. At least we were warmly dressed for winter- it was cold and windy too! The walk to the reservation normally took us an hour and a half. After about an hour after we left, the wind started to blow and then the snow came. Soon it was a driving blizzard. Thankfully, we were able to follow the railroad tracks, carefully listening for any trains that might be coming (the wind and driving snow masked noise). When we finally came to where we thought Indian Joe's tepee was, we turned off and in a few minutes, were hopelessly lost in the blinding snow. We decided it was wisest to just build a lean-to and wait the snowstorm out for the night. We had also been smart enough to mark a trail through the woods on our way there in case Indian Joe came looking for us or we were forced to find our way back. So, we settled in, started a fire, and made a lot of noise to scare off any bears that might be close by.

We were lucky. Indian Joe was expecting us and when the snow started, he had set out to find our trail. He was a superb woodsman, but even he had trouble with this massive storm. He found our marks on the trees and followed them to our fire. It's an understatement to say we were ecstatic to see him! With his help we built a proper shelter and waited out the storm, secure in the knowledge that an expert outdoorsman was with us. The blizzard lasted all night. The next day, Indian Joe decided it would be best to head for town to allay the fear of Mr. Rancia and our friends. Halfway back to Depot Harbor, we met a search party that had set out from town that morning looking for us. They had even considered setting out the night before, but understandably waited for daylight and the snow to stop. Everyone was convinced we had been hopelessly lost and might be found dead and frozen. Thanks to Indian Joe we survived, none the less for wear.

Indian Joe was one of the rare breed of independent people who refused to live in a town. He lived alone in the "bush", hunting and trapping to eke out an existence inspired by a love of freedom. Many of these men were Indians or half-breeds, the children of mixed parenthood. These kinds of men vanished gradually over the years. I doubt if there are very many, if any, "Indian Joe's" still around.

EDITOR'S NOTE: Pop dictated this before we started seeing homeless people in the streets of our major cities. In a sense, these are the "Indian Joes" of today. I don't think Pop was so much commenting on the fact that they are Indians or half-breeds so much as they were free spirits who did not want to conform to living in rooms, houses, or apartments.

I'm not ashamed to admit that I was frightened that night. Not to be frightened would have been foolish. But Billy and I kept our heads, followed the rules and survived. Would we have done so without Indian Joe? I don't know. At the time, and since, I just accepted the grace of a loving God to bring me through my peril. Needless to say, after this incident we were much more careful on our treks through the woods. There was always the threat of danger about us in the wilderness of Depot Harbor.

That fall, just after the war ended, tragedy struck when Mr. Rancia took Billy on a hunting trip one weekend. He had lectured to Billy about the need to be cautious with a gun, but often boys of sixteen only half listen to instructions. Unfortunately, Billy had to live with the burden of his horrific mistake for the rest of his life. After he and his father had been in the woods for a while, Mr. Rancia had to return to the lodge for something, leaving Billy on his own. A short time later, Billy heard the sound of movement and rustling leaves in the woods. Though his father had left him with strict orders not to shoot anything until he returned, Billy didn't want to miss his big chance to shoot his first buck all by himself. He waited until the sound got closer, and then fired. Billy ran over to inspect his target and stared in horror and disbelief- he had shot and killed his own father.

Mr. Rancia was survived by his wife and five children. This number doesn't include me, though I too felt like I had lost a father. It was the kind of incredible tragedy that Mrs. Rancia was never able to get over. A few months later, she sold the hotel and moved to Huntsville, Ontario. I tried to keep contact with them but found that we drifted further and further apart with time. It went from letters to Christmas cards to the occasional card. Billy had a hard time coping with the killing. I heard from him about ten years after and I got the impression he was okay, but I really wondered. Accidents that become tragedies heal with time, but never really disappear.

CHAPTER FOUR

LEARNING ABOUT LIFE
"AFTER THE WAR"

Aside from my encounter with the officials on the train questioning whether I was a draft-dodger, the First World War affected my life in other, more subtle ways. I spent most of the war years in Depot Harbor and life up to that point had been good. The city was safe and clean. People could sleep at night with their doors unlocked. Everyone was courteous and friendly. The people of Depot Harbor, and Toronto as well, were like one big grown-up family to me. I've always felt those days in Depot Harbor were the golden days of my life.

However, by 1918 the war was finally winding down. The United States had at last entered the war in the spring of 1917 and following spring, its impact was being felt. There was a great feeling of optimism in the air. Everyone in Canada felt that the war would soon be over. During this time, some of the war veterans were beginning to return home. What a strange term- "Veterans"- for young men, most in their early twenties, little older than me. As I neared my own eighteenth birthday, I too faced the prospect of being drawn into military service. While I already believed strongly in pacifism, I was still quite prepared to serve if I were called upon to do so.

It was so sad what war did to such brave soldiers. These young men, wounded, crippled, missing an arm or leg- this was what the people of Canada saw as our "boys" returned from war. Seeing this tragedy myself has always affected me and my opinion about how war is inflicted on the young. I remember meeting many of the returning veterans to Depot Harbor. They were all touched in some way by what they had lived through. As someone just a few years younger, I heard them talk of the brutality and senseless killing, the overwhelming feeling of hopelessness, their rejection of the so-called "glory of war". They suffered through all kinds of wounds and injury, shrapnel attacks, being mustard gassed, the new and frightening killing technology of tanks and airplanes, and the sheer cold, devastatingly impersonal nature of being a meaningless cog caught up in a great power struggle. My friend John came back without a leg; another friend, Michael, had his lungs permanently scarred by gas; and my good friend Jack was blind in one eye. I thanked God that I had been spared from going to war, and resolved forever to do what I could to stop war from ever happening again. These assaults on my emotions and good sense have always remained with me.

Later in my life, it bothered me that the technology of death used to brutalize soldiers in World War I became a factor in brutalizing civilians, as well as soldiers, in World War II. Suffice to say we must all be vigilant to prevent violence and conflict, since future wars would undoubtedly be that much worse. Children and innocent citizens seem to be increasingly used as pawns in armed conflicts. Somewhere, somehow, we have to stop this trend.

Still, despite the horrors of modern warfare, I'll never be able to forget World War I. So many people were permanently injured, both physically and mentally. It used to turn my insides thinking about what a great loss it was to cripple so many men and waste so many lives. It was such a high price to pay- for what? Like the United States, Canada hadn't been directly involved with the war and to make matters worse, many of these poor soldiers had been volunteers. It just reinforced my belief that nobody wins anything from war. Ultimately, war is just for those who want more power, and to this day, I can't understand why it continues to exist.

I'm also a Roman Catholic who believes in Christ's teachings. I try to adhere to God's Commandments and as far as I'm concerned, "Thou shalt not kill" is not something to be conveniently discarded when countries can find no other solution to their disputes. It always nagged at me that if I had been forced to go to war, I would have been required to obey an officer who would train me to kill or be killed. Again, I'm thankful I was never placed in such a situation where I'd have to choose between my country and my God.

In addition to all these sorrows of war, there is the never-ending sense of pointlessness surrounding the grief and depth of loss to the families of those dead and injured soldiers. It's so unbearably hard for mothers and fathers to have their sons fight valiantly on the front line just to have them die anyway. It astounds me at times that we, as modern, "civilized" people, would actually go out onto a battlefield to kill one another.

I had just turned eighteen when World War I officially ended. The Armistice brought much needed peace at long last and there were celebrations in every town. People were literally dancing in the streets over the "victory". I remember how confused I was by this. How could people condone killing and destruction and then celebrate it afterwards? How could they be <u>happy</u> after four years of murder? It didn't seem right. It didn't seem proper or respectful! Though I later understood the real excitement arose from everyone's relief and joy that the fighting was over, I never understood the need for it to have ever started in the first place.

Life all over Canada was drastically upset and chaotic after the Armistice. So much death from the war almost seemed to have created a germ in the atmosphere; severe Spanish flu cases were developing all over the world, even in our own sheltered Depot Harbor, causing hundreds, if not thousands, of deaths everyday. It was frightening how quickly this flu killed people. One day you'd have the sniffles, two days later you were in a coffin. It struck without warning. Perfectly healthy people would suddenly complain of headaches, sore legs, or uncontrollable coughing. Everyone was at risk; it didn't matter who- the young, the old, or anyone in between. Whole families became ill, or maybe just a few. Many died. Everyone was scared. It was awful how that virus could spread, too. The Spanish flu was ferociously contagious[1].

---

[1] Spanish influenza. During the fall and winter of 1918–19, Canada (including Newfoundland and Labrador) suffered approximately 50,000 deaths in a pandemic of influenza that took approximately 21 million lives worldwide. Thought at the time to have originated in Spain, the disease probably started in Canton, was carried to Europe by Chinese trench diggers, and was spread to North America by soldiers returning from the Great War. Flu flourished in army camps and rapidly spread across the

When the flu epidemic began, there was no doctor living in Depot Harbor. Luckily, however, a Presbyterian minister who had been doing missionary work in China- and just happened to be a medical doctor- was in town visiting friends. He was also staying at the hotel where I was working at the time. The minister became Depot Harbor's savior during this crisis.

The hotel was substituting as kind of a makeshift hospital (the town hospital was overflowing with patients) and was packed with sick people. I frequently looked after them when I wasn't in the kitchen.

I ran errands for the ill, secured cough medicine, delivered meals, cleaned them and their rooms when they vomited or soiled themselves, and generally did whatever I could to help. There were also times when I had the unpleasant job of helping to bury those people who died. I felt I was strong, young, and invincible. I prayed to God thanking Him for my continued good health and for the opportunity to help the sick to recover. But despite my and the hotel staff's efforts, many of our guests were dying. We eventually lost about eight people from the hotel.

Of course, the doctor and I got to know one another well throughout all this and he constantly

---

continent along all transportation routes. Despite attempts at quarantine, no part of the country escaped infection. The isolated communities along Labrador's coast were probably the hardest hit, losing perhaps a third of their population. There were no effective drugs for either prevention or cure.

Source: Janice Dickin "Spanish influenza" *The Oxford Companion to Canadian History.* Ed. Gerald Hallowell. Oxford University Press, 2004. *Oxford Reference Online.* Oxford University Press.

advised me to "be careful". This was an extremely potent flu and I was in contact with a lot of very sick people. Medicine being what it was in the early 1900's, he told me to chew tobacco and drink a little whiskey as often as I could. "Be careful, don't eat too much, and keep your bowels open. That way, you might avoid the flu." Luckily, God spared my life and I never did catch the disease. But looking back, I think it had to do more with my youth and overall good health than the good doctor's advice.

Because this wonderful Christian man spent countless hours with a town full of sick and dying people, he had little time to look after his own health. He, too, became ill, dying shortly afterwards. I looked after him while he was sick, and felt so bad when he passed away that I cried. Many, many people owed their lives to this unselfish devoted man. He was one of the most selfless individuals I've ever met- an inspirational human being who devoted his life to God and God's children. I always found it sad and ironic that he died in the midst of those he saved.

In the spring of 1919 I decided it was time to leave Depot Harbor. While I had been happy during most of the four years I spent there, I wanted to leave my recent sad memories behind me. I also wanted to pursue my desire to become a chef. I thought of returning to Toronto, but read that the flu epidemic was even more severe there. Years later I learned from my wife's Uncle Tony, who was a soldier in the Army, that the flu was so bad in that city that army wagons collected the bodies for mass burial.

I decided it was best to avoid Toronto and instead chose to travel to the town of North Bay where my Uncle Michael (the minister) now lived. I took the

Grand Trunk Railway all the way to Ottawa, not knowing where I was going or how I was going to live. I also found out that people had strange customs in northern Ontario. Different hotels had their own staff trying to get passengers off the train; they'd all be standing on the platform shouting for people to come to their establishment. Each hotel also had a bus drawn by two horses that could carry twelve or fourteen passengers. I asked the first boy who approached me if his hotel was a nice place. He said it was lovely- he was French. I gave my bag to him and got in the bus.

A few more passengers came in and sat with me. The driver then got in and clucked to the horses to get them moving. We arrived at a hotel on Main Street that wasn't very far from the station. It was a nice, commercial hotel with a bar, and it was clean. They gave me a comfortable room and I decided to eat supper there. There weren't many people in the dining room, only about twenty or twenty-five. I had to wait so long for supper that I asked why there was such a delay. A "Mr. Matthews" was the owner and apparently Mrs. Matthews was in the kitchen, doing all the cooking. They were having trouble because the chef had just quit. What a stroke of luck! Of course, I immediately told them what experience I had. He offered me the job and the next thing I knew I was the chef at the Hotel.

The responsibilities of chef at a hotel consisted of much more than short order cooking. Every day I prepared breakfast, along with baking several pies and preparing soup, a roast and a variety of supper entrees. Though it was a busy restaurant- serving about five hundred people per day- I was the only cook, assisted by just one kitchen helper and a dishwasher. Hotel work was hard work (harder than I thought!) Yet I wasn't really learning any new techniques of my trade. Dissatisfied and tired, I decided to hunt for a more challenging job further north and made plans to go to Timmons, Ontario.

Timmons was a small town compared to Toronto but certainly much bigger than Depot Harbor. It was a major mining town in northern Ontario and a major stop on the railroad. Its true fame came from the fact that it was the site of so many gold mines. But it certainly was "out in the wilds", and while not backward, it certainly was a small town. For its day, it could be considered the frontier. All the way on the train to Timmons, I saw a lot of bush fires. I wondered what was going on because it looked as though whole towns had been burned! I started getting worried; what was I doing up here? I arrived in Timmons wondering if there would be bush fires there too but it appeared to be a nice town and everyone was busy. I was hungry when I got off the train and as I left the station, I saw a big covered wagon with six wheels. It was a luncheon wagon with about fifteen stools inside and a nice lunch counter, so I sat down. I enjoyed a nice hot breakfast and got talking to "Joe", a Frenchman who ran the lunch wagon.

From childhood, I was a born mimic with a special flair for languages. Already I had learned some French from my days in Depot Harbor, as well as some Polish, Ukrainian, Greek and Chinese. Years later, when my son, Rocky, was studying German, I decided to learn along with him. This flair for languages helped me in my job searches. It was also much easier to speak to people in their native tongue if they were having difficulty with English.

Anyway, Joe told me in French how busy they were and that it was interesting work. I told him about my workings as a chef and that I was good on short orders. Again, my luck held out! He said I was just the man he was looking for; they did a lot of short order work and needed a second cook to help out at the lunch wagon.

So, I got a job and a place to stay all in one day. I thoroughly enjoyed working for Joe. I got to know the folks in town and felt right at home. The bad part of living in Timmons came in August when the temperature rose into the upper 80's and dried everything out. A spark of lightening could set fire to the bush instantly. Later that summer, there were some people there who had been careless with matches who finally did cause a bush fire. This time, it wasn't far from Timmons. It was six miles away in all directions around the town and closing fast. The fire fighters tried to stop it but were afraid that the outskirts of town would still be burned. Some of the trains started evacuating people. I didn't know what to do- I could leave town, but the stations weren't allowing people to take their belongings on the train. Fortunately, just as I was debating whether or not to just abandon my trunk and run, the wind shifted, a rainstorm arrived and the town was saved.

On the other hand, it was very cold in Timmons in the winter. It often reached fifty below zero there. Early that spring, as the ice and snow started to break up, I thought to myself how terrible the weather was- either extreme heat or bitter cold. You risked getting burned by bush fires in the summer or frozen in the winter! I started having second thoughts about staying there for the long term, so Joe and I parted as good friends and I headed once again back to Toronto.

My movement from job to job like this was fueled in part by ambition and a streak of independence. I also like to believe it was based on a sense of leadership, of striking out "ahead of the pack". Making choices and taking chances is all part of the game of life and I suppose I played it to a bit of an extreme as a teenager. I don't think my need for independence was particularly normal in someone my age, but maybe it was just the times. Many young men my age in Canada were on their own and chasing their dreams too.

So, of course, in Toronto the first thing I did was to go to an employment office and seek work as a chef. Unfortunately, the only job the interviewer had available was in a lumberjack camp seven miles from Smooth Rock Falls, Ontario. This position would require the preparation of four meals a day for eighteen men. This sounded like a lot of hard work, but the pay of one hundred and twenty-five dollars a month was too tempting. "Well," I thought, "it certainly would be different!" I decided to take a chance and left the next morning with five other prospective chefs headed for Smooth Rock Falls. All the other men had worked at lumber camps before, so they quickly let me in on the "finer points" of outdoor life.

To this day I still laugh at the sight I must have presented. Can you imagine someone showing up in a lumber camp in the wilderness wearing only brown patent leather pumps and a fedora as a hat, bringing with him one wool and one cotton sweater as warm clothing, and not owning a stitch of padded or quilted underwear! While I did have a winter coat, it was certainly more suited for city life than tramping through the mud and bush of the forest. Needless to say, I gave off the image of a pampered city slicker instead of an experienced rough and tumble lumber camp cook (or chef as I preferred to think). What a change from working in a hotel kitchen! It's a wonder my five companions were able to keep a straight face without laughing.

They were kind enough, however, to tell me I would need new clothes, and that I could buy them in the company store at the camp. What they didn't tell me was that I would be charged an arm and a leg for them. That was typical business then: soak your workers for items they need to live and do their jobs, charge them as much as possible and as a result, you get employees who are forced to work longer and longer hours for your company in order to pay their bills. In some cases, I don't believe this was done out of spite or greed so much as out of economic necessity. Profit margins were not large in lumbering. And while the prices were higher in the company store, it did provide a service for the people in the camps. In any event, I was so cold at that point that I didn't particularly care about the price.

It seemed the only good thing about the start of this new career was that I picked the spring to do it in. Thank God I didn't land there in the middle of winter. My experiences in Depot Harbor had given me enough sense to avoid that. Still, I was cold. Even though it was spring, the temperature was usually below zero! My friends from the train were right about me. Never in my life have I been that cold.

As you probably know, lumber jacking consists of cutting down trees- usually big ones. In those days, only axes and saws were used. There were no gasoline engine powered saws like today. The work was and still is physically demanding and dangerous. No matter how careful a tree is "set" to fall, there is no guarantee that it will do as planned. Endless days of sawing wood and hauling lumber could run a man's health into the ground. Because of this, the lumberjacks themselves were a unique breed of strong, hardy, agile men who faced solitary lives without fear or complaint. Life was also very primitive for the lumberjacks. There was nothing else for them to do except work, eat, and sleep. They all tried to work the longest hours possible to make as much money as they could in a short time. Their only entertainment was the log rolling games they had, drinking, and playing cards. Needless to say, meals were an important part of their relaxation, as well as being vital for their continued well being and strength on the job.

The lumberjacks normally walked or were taken on sleds pulled by teams of large draft horses to their assigned cutting areas. They worked singly or in teams to cut down their quota of trees. The same horse sleds were later used to pull the fresh logs from where they were cut down to the river. In the winter time, these stacks of logs would freeze together. The lumberjacks would have to break them up with dynamite in order to float the timber downstream in the spring. Everything was hard. Living was dangerous. This was the kind of brutal environment into which I arrived in the late spring of 1918.

I found out there were actually seven camps in all when I arrived for work. The center camp was the main one, with three to the left and three more to the right. Each chef would be assigned to his own camp. In order to arrive at the different locations, we would have to travel by canoe across a river several miles long and a quarter of a mile wide. All of us went to the main camp first that day, where the head chef gave us our instructions. Meal times were to be at 5:30 am, 10:30 am, 3:30 p.m. and 7:00 p.m. Each of us would be given an abundance of beef and salt pork that we could prepare in any variety of ways.

Fried salt pork, which tasted much like bacon, was to be always served at the first morning meal. At 10:30, the men were to have a main course of steak. Certain foods had to be present on the table at all times: fruit, Johnnycakes (pancakes) and syrup, jam and jellies, and bread and butter. I knew how to make all of these except bread. I told the head chef I had never baked bread and he got very annoyed. "What are you doing here then?" he yelled. I explained that the employment agency never mentioned bread-baking skills were necessary for the job; otherwise I would never have taken it. The head chef finally agreed to supply the bread for my camp until he could teach me to bake it myself. What an introduction to my new job!

I was stationed at Camp #2, and tried my best to keep up with the hectic meal schedule and learning to bake bread, but I only lasted a month and a half. I suppose I just wasn't right for the job. My day began at 4:30 and went until the end of supper at 7:00. It wasn't really the long hours that made me decide to quit my job; I just couldn't get used to living in the wild outdoors. Our living accommodations were very basic. The bunkhouses were made of logs and the cracks between them were filled with hardened mud. They were always noisy, smelly and full of men either drinking, playing cards, squabbling, or snoring. The water pump was usually frozen, leaving melted snow as our only source of water. Of course, there was also no indoor plumbing and I was back to using an outhouse again. I'm a little embarrassed to admit I was afraid of the animals that lived in the woods: bear, moose, raccoon, deer and skunk, as well as numerous forms of biting bugs. It was not a friendly place.

Oh, how I longed for a warm, safe enclosed kitchen back in civilization! I went to the head chef and told him I wanted to leave. In reality, he was a kind man who had tried to help me. He well recognized that I belonged in a city instead of the outdoors. He even suggested I try working on the railroad as a chef.

I thought that was a good idea, so I applied and was accepted. All of a sudden, I went from being a tough-living lumber camp cook to a prestigious dining car chef. The work was much easier to deal with, but the constant motion of the railroad car proved as difficult to handle as the bugs, bears, and cold of the lumber camps. I decided once more to return to Toronto.

EDITOR'S NOTE: Pop always had a twinkle in his eye when talking about the lumber camps and the railroad. I don't know if it was so much being nineteen or being in the frontier. I think it was much of both. I think Pop was happy for having done it, but equally happy that he left.

It was the fall of 1919 when I arrived in Toronto. I got a room in the same building I had lived in when I first came to Canada, and secured a job at the old Superior Lunch Restaurant as a short order cook at night. There I was, almost six years after I had arrived in Canada as a young immigrant from Modugno, working as a cook in the great city of Toronto and feeling right at home. I made pies after midnight, and worked from eight in the evening to eight in the morning- twelve hours a day, seven days a week. I got paid well though. Thirty dollars a week was big money in 1920 (the average factory worker made about ten or twelve dollars a week). I didn't mind the long hours; I was young and working towards my future

As I grew from youth to manhood, I saw myself changing from a somewhat frightened needy boy to an adventurous, hard-working independent young man. Along the way, I was blessed with having made wise choices. For this I'll always thank my parents who prepared me to be honest, practical and responsible. Whenever I faced real problems, I carried on conversations with my parents in my mind. I would imagine listening to their advice, though often I didn't like it. But I mentally listened, judged, and then did what I felt was right. In that way, I finally became an adult.

One of the most important things I ever learned was that you have to respect all people if you want to be respected yourself. You cannot receive what you do not give. In life, everyone has a duty to perform or a role to fulfill. That's what work and education are all about. And people have to respect the right and responsibility of others to do their jobs, whether its being a policeman, a parent, an artist, an engineer, a plumber, or a secretary. I also believe it's important to maintain respect for those who've lost their jobs or are unable to perform their duties because of illness, tragedy or age. You never know when you might be in their same circumstances.

All of us face life as a gamble. All of us are down on our luck sometimes. But those who are willing to take on adult responsibility survive, where those who still think like children look for parents to bail them out, whether the "parents" be real parents, the government, friends or society. I always prided myself on trying to act as an adult and relate to others as an adult.

I am also grateful that I was brought up with the traditional middle class values. I was raised with an ethic of hard work, waiting for rewards in life, patiently working towards far-off goals, and personal sacrifice (especially for family). I understand that a person is what his or her family and culture teaches them to be. As a result, I am eternally grateful for the kind of positive, wholesome work and family oriented beliefs I was exposed to as a child. However, I also believe that life tests all of us only to the limit of our abilities. If we are tested beyond this limit, then we are sure to get help from family, friends or God, but only if we ask! If we never ask for help, then we fail before we even start.

I've always felt that self-examination- taking an inventory of yourself- was an important part of living, too. How can you act as a responsible adult or relate well to the other people in your life (even strangers) if you don't know what your strengths, weaknesses, thoughts, and beliefs are? Knowing what's truly important and accepting yourself and your life can make it much easier to respect and understand how everyone else around feels. Some people, like me, are lucky enough to have family and close friends to help them in this task. Others may find help in counseling or therapy. Still, others may find their source of guidance in God. Whenever I was at a total loss for what to do, I found getting down on my knees and praying always worked. It's a shame more young people don't try prayer and self-examination. Maybe if they did, the world's future would be a happier, more loving place- a place without theft, envy, selfishness or violence.

I suppose life is just basically give and take. There always seems to be a struggle for balance among people. These values and beliefs I describe have been important to me and have worked in my life. I don't claim, nor do I believe, they will work the same way for everyone because we all have our own set of problems, priorities and solutions. I sincerely hope, however, that some of my thoughts and experiences can help others as they cope with life's challenges.

What have I done, specifically, to help make my decisions in life? First of all, I always lived by my family's tradition of setting aside money according to need. Out of three dollars, one would go to pay the debts of the past by looking after my parents, one paid the costs of the present by looking after my wife and me, and the third was for investing in the future by looking after my children. I've never believed in having mass or idle wealth merely as a sign of importance. Great wealth that is used to oppress- or impress others- seems senseless. Wealth is best used to help others, whether by creating jobs, providing education or simply providing people opportunities to help themselves. After all, isn't that what we're all on this earth for? To care for one another?

During my lifetime, I have faced death, illness, being broke, despair, loneliness, and most other forms of human misery. I don't think it's possible for any of us to avoid these things. However, it's interesting that philosophers have noted that 10% of life results from things you cannot control- but the other 90% results from your attitude towards them. My attitude has always been upbeat and optimistic no matter how badly I felt. There were many times maintaining a positive outlook was the last thing I wanted to do. But I disciplined myself to avoid the tempting cloak of self-imposed misery. It would have been so easy to just give in to it. I would always remind myself eventually that there was enough trouble and misery in the world without my seeking it.

Lastly, I have always made a special effort to contribute, in whatever small ways I could- to my community and society in general. I feel it's vital to be a productive citizen, whether through paid or volunteer work, or just "getting involved". Whatever your skill or talent might be, you can produce something or make things happen to help others survive on this planet. All my life, I've felt proud to work. There was always a sense of duty and purpose in my life and I fulfilled that purpose. I gladly gave my share of love and labor and in return, took my fair share of life's rewards.

EDITOR'S NOTE: Right on, Pop! Yes, you were lucky to have such an industrious, sensible, and loving family to teach you successful values and ethics. As his son, I feel fortunate to have grown up with the same strong family network. It's because of this belief in family that I hope this book can serve as an example to others.

"APPRECIATING DIFFERENCES"

When the war was over, I was free to return to my hometown in Italy. But Modugno wasn't "home" anymore. (To this day, I still feel Canada is the place where I grew up). I was still caught up in the adventure of a primitive land…in the excitement of exploring Canada. The only drawback I had to face was loneliness. Though I had made many new friends, they couldn't replace my own family. I missed my parents. I longed to see my brothers and sisters. If I couldn't bring myself to go back to Italy, then I would try my best to bring Italy here.

So that's just what I did. Five months after I started working at "Superior Lunch", my brother, Frank, came from the "old country". Frank had always been my side kick growing up and it was great to have him with me. We would sit by the hour and talk about all the things we used to do. He was a welcome addition to our family group in Toronto.

I was even able to get him a job at the restaurant as a night helper. As time went on, I wanted to continue spending time with Frank but my job wasn't challenging enough to warrant my staying. I guess my adventurous streak was showing too. It was 1921 and I had been in Canada for seven years working my way up the culinary ladder. Advancement was not a quick process and it had already taken all these years to move up the ladder from dish-washer to full-fledged chef. So, the following spring, I told Frank I'd strike out for both of us and try to find a place in Windsor, Ontario for him to join me. I would only be six hours away by rail and promised to keep in touch. While I hated leaving my brother, I also knew I couldn't pass up the opportunity to move ahead.

In Italy, we had always spoken of people as being emigrants to "America". There was never any distinction made between Canada and the United States. Though I'm well aware of the separation between the two countries today, I feel as much at home in the United States as I do in Canada because I spent so many years crossing back and forth between them. When I was settled in Windsor, I worked as a chef at a small hotel that was close to the United States border. Frequently on weekends I would venture into Detroit,

Michigan by ferry boat with some of my co-workers. I thoroughly enjoyed these trips and started thinking I might really like working in the States. The immigration fee at the time was only $8, an amount that would enable me to stay and work in the U.S. as long as I wished.

EDITOR'S NOTE: Pop was not too clear on this point and I am not sure if this was an immigration fee or working paper visa fee. I got the distinct impression from my conversations with Pop that he actually had papers of the landed immigrant in the U.S. I have never gone back to check this, and never really discussed it in detail with him. It would be an interesting point if he had remained in the U.S.

Having no special ties in Windsor, I packed my bags and went to Detroit ready for another challenge. I was fortunate enough to get a room and a good job right away at a large Main Street restaurant that afforded me the opportunity to learn many new skills.

I love Canada, I love the United States and I love Italy. I love everybody. As far as I'm concerned, I have no enemies in this world. I believe I appreciate all people, no matter what their differences. Regardless of race, class or religion, my mother and Catholicism always taught me to love and respect my fellow man. We are all God's children. I hold no grudges against anyone and it's not my business to judge other people. Living in so many countries, in so many different towns and experiencing different cultures helped me to understand all kinds of people- although it could be that what I really learned was just how much the same we all are.

Anyway, the following year I received a phone call from Toronto that my brother-in-law, Tony Bungaro, had just arrived from Italy. He was the

husband of my older sister, Angelina. The Martino
family in Canada was growing at a slow but steady
pace! I felt obligated, but happy, to leave Detroit and
help secure lodgings and work for Tony in Toronto. In
those days it was difficult for me to let relatives stay by
themselves, especially since I was usually the one
sending them money for their passage in the first place.
Tony was a well-educated man in the Italian language
and soon got a job with a local Italian newspaper. But
he had to settle in and get used to a new country. Back
then, there weren't that many immigrants here.
Traveling from Europe and back means nothing today,
but in those days, it meant a great deal of change and
adjustment. After he was settled, I returned to Detroit
and got a new job with a big restaurant near the Ford
plant as a short order cook. It was a very busy place,
and I fit right in.

Let me add here that getting a job wasn't quite
as easy as I may seem to imply. Jobs, good jobs
especially were, then as now, not easy to get. For the
most part, I didn't have much trouble getting jobs
because I knew people in the restaurant business and
had a reputation for working hard and getting things
done. The restaurant community is a small one and for
young men like me, the way up the ladder was to seek
opportunity and move on, so long as it was upward. I
had a strong commitment to the work of being a chef, if
not necessarily while still moving upward, to the
specific establishment. I not only got jobs quickly, but
found it relatively easy to return to previous employers
at a higher level. As a cook, if you were advancing you
were in demand. My advice to young people today is to
strive to move upward, always do an outstanding job
wherever you are (or whatever you're doing), and

always leave on friendly terms with any employer. This approach always worked for me!

It could be said that I was always "in the right place at the right time". The same can be said of a hockey player who just happens to be at the side of the net, and lifts his stick in order to deflect the puck into the net for a goal. It is not luck that put the hockey player there, nor is it luck that gets him to raise the stick. You have to have a sense of what is going on around you and where the opportunities are. So it wasn't so much being "in the right place at the right time" as it was continually being aware of what was going on, where the jobs were, and how I might know of them. I always found throughout my life that continually working at something, digging, digging, digging- usually lead to some worthwhile result.

It was that kind of continual digging, and continual working at family relationships that kept us all together.

In the spring of 1923, Tony's wife, my sister Angelina, arrived in Toronto to join her husband. My brother-in-law wasn't yet experienced enough to get accommodations appropriate for his wife, in addition to having little extra money. So, again I left Detroit in support of my family and teamed up with Tony and my brother, Frank, to get a four room flat in Toronto. As always, we worked together, helping one another cope with our new lives in a new world. Angelina had a lot of news from Modugno that made me feel homesick. Her stories reminded me just how much I wanted to see my mother. I missed the rest of my family so much. Then and there, I made up my mind to pay a visit to everyone back in Modugno.

"GOING HOME"

On the 28th of that March, I proudly became a naturalized Canadian citizen. I was very happy; Canada was now my official home. In the meantime, I was back at the Superior Lunch again as a short order cook, once more making pies at night. However, my happiness over becoming a Canadian citizen didn't mean I had forgotten about my plans to go to Italy. Of course, I had kept in touch with my family since the time I arrived here ten years earlier. Many of my brothers and sisters were now with me in Canada, but I longed to be reunited with my parents. In late June of 1923, I wrote to my mother to tell her I was coming home at last!

After getting my passport, I booked passage to Italy on a boat called the Colombo. Because this was decades before transcontinental airline service, there was no direct route from Toronto to Italy and I had to make arrangements for traveling by rail to New York City, where the Colombo was to sail from.

When I arrived at the dock, I saw the ship was an older one, probably built at the turn of the century that had been newly refurbished. Obviously, the Colombo had served as a troop ship during the war. The conditions of my voyage were not much different than those on the Palermo when I crossed with my father in 1914. However, the trip went much faster this time. We made it from New York to Naples in eight days.

There were many friendly people on board that I got to know during the voyage; several of them were from Italy, too. Naturally, I spent much of my time with my fellow Italians, swapping stories about our homeland. My situation seemed to be unique, however, as I was such a young immigrant returning to Italy after nine years in America. To be honest, I think I was lionized by all the ladies with young daughters of marrying age. Their hints eventually did start me thinking about marriage. Even more startling, I suddenly realized that one of the reasons for this trip was not only to see my parents, but to get their help and approval in selecting a wife.

When the <u>Colombo</u> docked in Naples, all my new friends went their separate ways. I anxiously began searching the crowds for the familiar faces of my family and was not disappointed. The men folk were all there to greet me. I went home with them to Modugno and what a happy reunion there was that day! I had brought presents for everyone and was surprised to see how much my brothers and sisters had grown. I also saw for the first time my brother, Raffaele and my sister, Maria. For him I had a train set, and for her, the biggest teddy bear I could find. It was almost as big as me, and certainly bigger than the four year old sister who soon became my shadow. Little did I realize that in 1939 she would come to Canada as a nineteen year old woman to care for my two sons, and grow up more like my own daughter than my sister.

Needless to say, Mama and Papa were thrilled and very excited to see me. I couldn't tell them enough about my adopted home. The talk went on for hours that first evening in the bosom of my family. I can still see the happy faces of my parents and brothers and sisters hanging on my every word. This was something I would never forget!

Throughout my entire stay, Mama never got tired of cooking for me. She asked me every day what I wanted to eat. Papa took me all around town to visit, and encouraged me once more to remain and run the family business. World War I had affected Modugno's whole economy. While my father still owned some land, the wine business had permanently shrunk to one cantina and even that was much smaller. Papa was still the proud businessman, but I could see that he needed help. All of Italy was in the grip of the depression.

I decided to see what I could do to help. I bought a small farm and told my father it was his to use and manage for the rest of his life. Later, when both of my parents had died after the Second World War, I deeded the farm to my brothers and sisters in Italy to share equally. Doing this for my family made me feel like I was somehow repaying Mama and Papa who had done so much for me.

Italy, and Modugno itself, seemed a little smaller, dustier and backward then I remembered. I had waited all those years to return and was disappointed. I knew I could never live there again. My plan of returning only to visit had been justified. While I tried to convince my parents to return to Canada with me, I knew it was a lost hope. Their life was in Modugno, just as mine was in America.

Ironically, it was a war that had kept me from returning to Italy in 1914 and it was the possibility of another war, this time between Italy and Greece, which now forced me to leave, just three and a half months after my homecoming. There was anxious talk of Mussolini possibly declaring war on Greece because of the assassination of an Italian commissioner. Men were being recruited into the Italian Army left and right. I had to return to Canada as quickly as possible before I was drafted, too. As luck would have it, as I arrived in Naples to head home to Canada, there were soldiers on the ship asking to see everyone's discharge papers.

They asked for mine and acting like a tourist, I responded in English, "What did you say?" Since I had the benefit of being blonde and blue-eyed, they looked at my passport and must have decided I was British because they let me stay on the ship. (They weren't exactly the smartest fellows I'd ever met). I was lucky! If I'd been caught, I would have been forced into the Italian army, despite the fact that I was a British Canadian citizen. When it concerned the government of Italy, "Once an Italian; always an Italian." was the standard, at least when it came to army service and taxes.

In Italy, there was something called "universal military service". Every Italian male had to serve two years in the Army beginning at age eighteen (or later, if he had not served). There were no deferments for any reason whatsoever except for health restrictions; even then, almost everyone was judged physically able- that is, of course, unless special influence or bribes could be used. I was always opposed to serving, not out of fear, but because I despised the military and war and death. I saw then, and now, no reason for rational people to kill each other simply because someone in authority tells them to. If my family or home were threatened, no-one would be fiercer than I in defending those I loved. But war is wrong. Surely there are better answers than shooting it out. That's why I believe so strongly in what the United Nations tries to do today. As long as people can talk, killing can be avoided.

During the Second World War, both my sons were involved in military activities, and I was proud of them. Jack was in the Canadian Army Dental Corps and Rocky, attending a military high school, was a Cadet Officer. I loved them for their strong convictions, and of course, they had my blessing. I would never have been able to do what they did because during my whole childhood, I grew up loathing the military.

EDITOR'S NOTE: When Pop died in December of 1982, my oldest son, Peter was in his second year at the U.S. Naval Academy. He graduated with merit in 1985 and spent five years serving on nuclear submarines. My father would have been proud of Peter, even though he wouldn't have understood Peter's choice. In my own case, when I told him I wanted to apply for a commission in the Air Force, he gave me his blessing. When I changed my mind to pursue studies in Aerospace Sciences, he gave me his blessing once again, but with a sigh of relief.

For my brother Jack, his military service epitomized Pop's idea of stupidity. Though Jack was eventually a commissioned officer in the Dental Corps, at summer training, despite the fact that he would soon be a dentist, he was chosen to be an MP because he was also a burly football player. A Chinese classmate was appointed a camp cook because he was Chinese. This kind of pigeonholing that was prevalent in the Canadian military up until the fifties just reinforced Pop's low opinion of the military mind.

Earlier in Pop's life, the experience of his younger brother, Ralph, just added more fuel to his fire. In 1936, Ralph was inducted for service in the Italian Army and sent to fight in Ethiopia. The Martino family was strongly anti-fascist and anti-Mussolini, a dangerous political stance at the time. Uncle Ralph served his time, returning to Italy as a Sergeant. Though he had been released when his two years of service were over, Ralph was recalled in 1940 when Italy declared war on the Allies. This time, he was sent to Africa again and stationed in Libya. His unit was absorbed into the German Africa Corps and when Italy surrendered in 1943, he was placed in a detention camp by the Germans. Uncle Ralph somehow escaped, made his way to Egypt, and fought as an Italian co-belligerent against the Germans until the war ended.

Pop's Uncle Joe experienced similar mistreatment by the Italian Army. Uncle Joe emigrated to Toronto in 1905 and then went to California to invest heavily in vineyards. He eventually returned to Toronto, later traveling to Italy to visit the family. Upon his arrival, Uncle Joe was immediately inducted into the Italian Army since he had never served his required two years.

When World War I started, he was sent to the Austrian front where he served as a machine gun platoon leader and eventually became the Sergeant-Major of the regiment. In 1916 he was captured and spent almost two years in prison, close to starvation. Uncle Joe escaped early in 1918 and made his way back to the Italian lines. He was decorated for bravery, but sent back to the front anyway until the war ended. As would be expected, when he returned to the United States in 1919, he found that all of his vineyards had been taken over by the banks.

All of these incidents, together with Pop's strong feelings about violence and killing are what essentially turned him into a pacifist. I'm sure his priest uncles and Uncle Michael, the minister, had a great impact on him, his opinions, and his outlook on life.

CHAPTER FIVE

SETTLING DOWN
"CHALLENGES IN AMERICA:
STARTING A FAMILY"

After my homecoming in Modugno, I started thinking more about having a family of my own. At the age of 23, I felt I was finally ready for marriage. I also wanted to learn more about America and on the voyage back in the steamer, decided to try living in the United States again- this time in the town of Buffalo, New York.

I had no trouble getting into the States and took the train directly from New York City to Buffalo. As I got out of the train station in Buffalo, I thought I'd just take a streetcar to ride through the town and survey perspective restaurants and hotels, even though I didn't know where I was going. About this time, people were getting out of work and the streetcar was full of people, so I grabbed one of the straps that you could hold onto while standing in the aisle. Unbelievably, I noticed a familiar face standing next to me- a fellow childhood schoolmate of mine from Modugno, Vic Gramarosa. I explained to him that I had only just arrived in Buffalo a few hours earlier. Naturally, Vic insisted I go with him and he would find me a nice place to stay at the home of one of his neighbors. Ironically, it was the home of Ralph Trentadeau, a third cousin of my mother's. They did happen to have an empty room, so they took me in. That night we all had a party and it was as if I had gone home again. They treated me so wonderfully, just like my own family. It was a joyous and memorable reunion.

The Trentadeau's continued to offer me lodging in their home for the next few months and I appreciably accepted. I enjoyed their company as well as Vic's, with whom I spent many a night on the town, but my days were busily occupied with the duties of chef at a seafood house on Main Street. Later that spring, another of my brothers, Michael, arrived in Canada. Saying goodbye to my friends in Buffalo, I dutifully returned to Toronto once more to welcome him.

By then, I was able to get a house with my sister and brothers. It was a nice family group, the six of us. Angelina and Tony even had a son! We all got along fine and I loved helping to look after my nephew. I started seriously thinking about getting married again. I decided that all this running around was no good. Plus, I always enjoyed children and was looking forward to having some of my own.

I dated a lot, but didn't seem able to find anyone I wanted to spend the rest of my life with. It wasn't so much that I was particular, but being an independent sort, I wanted someone who was both understanding and patient, and independent as well. I also kept a little rule in mind. If I had to puzzle over whether or not I should marry a certain girl, then I knew she wasn't for me. I knew true love would show me the right person the moment I met her.

During this time, I became very friendly with Donald DiGiulio. Donald was very active in the Italian community as someone to turn to whenever papers or forms had to be filled out. Don had been educated by a private tutor and had much more than the equivalent of a high school education. This made him a very educated man in the Toronto of the 1920's. He was an energetic young man, who had been well educated in Italy and had his head screwed on right. He was known for helping out fellow immigrants and had helped me plan my trip to Italy. Upon my return, we started socializing again. Don had two younger brothers and an older sister living in Toronto, who had all been well educated, too. The DiGiulio family claimed to be direct descendants of Julius Caesar; I have to admit, Donald did appear to resemble some of the ancient sculptures of Caesar!

At one point, Don invited me home to meet his family. Though years later I kidded him that he had an ulterior motive in introducing me to his sister, he always insisted he wasn't the matchmaker type. He had assumed we'd like each other instantly because he knew us both so well. He was right. With his sister, Josephine (or "Peppinella" as we all called her, since it is the diminutive of Josephine, just as Betty is the diminutive of Elizabeth), it was love at first sight. Dating in those days was very restrictive; we were never really alone until we were married. Still, we managed to sneak a few private moments together-enough for us to exchange our affection for one another and for Josephine to consent to be my wife. By Christmas of 1924, we were engaged to be married.

Peppinella was a lovely young woman, with a charming personality, red hair and green eyes. She was also a fun loving girl, who had a winning smile and a joyful laugh. She found humor in everything. Her buoyant nature matched mine, so it was easy for us to have fun together. No wonder we fell in love so quickly! However, Peppinella had something I didn't have- infinite patience. Peppinella worked in a candy store as a salesgirl. She had also, like me, arrived in Canada at a young age and spoke flawless English.

We both wanted lots of children. I had come from a family of eight brothers and sisters, and she from four (her father died from pneumonia at thirty-three; otherwise, I'm sure she would have had a bigger family). I was terribly in love with her. At last, I would be surrounded by family again, this time my own.

On April 23, 1925, we were married in a Catholic wedding Mass in the sanctuary of St. Agnes' Church in Toronto. My brother, Frank, was my best man. The ceremony was beautiful…and so was Josephine. How lucky I was to be marrying such a wonderful woman. Mass was followed by an intimate celebration dinner for both families back at the house. Angelina prepared the meal and homemade wine. Since this was during Prohibition, alcohol was permitted only in private homes and could not be sold. After dinner, we went to the church hall for the reception with about two hundred guests. Cakes, fancy sandwiches and fruits were served along with soft drinks. Though it was a "dry" reception, we all sang and danced anyway having a thoroughly enjoyable time.

Our honeymoon was a two-week vacation spent in breathtaking cities of Ottawa and Montreal. In those days, it was rare for anyone to travel any distance for an extended period of time; most people simply couldn't afford it. Our honeymoon was a fun and fulfilling experience- the beginning of a beautiful relationship with memories I've always treasured.

Because Peppinella was a redhead and I was fair-skinned, no one who met us ever took us for Italian. We found it amusing to suddenly switch from English to Italian, seeing the surprise on the faces of our friends. We'd leave for work together, sharing our money and joy. I still remember one morning when we rounded up all our loose change so we'd each have enough for the streetcar. In the cash society of the time, the cost of buying furniture and setting up housekeeping often led to instances of "matching pennies" to meet the needs of the day. Our life was simple, but full of loving relationships with family and friends.

I became very close with Josephine's family. Every Sunday we would have a big family get-together. Peppinella always had her three brothers there with whom I soon formed a quartet, playing horseshoes and "briscola" (an Italian card game similar to 500 rummy). We also tried to spend free time with friends of ours, at least as much as was possible within the confines of my six and a half day work week. Now that I was married, I did my best to work two short days per week where I could leave at five or six in the evening. Of course, I had to work longer on other days to make up for the time I took off.

Our marriage was a partnership in every way. When Peppinella became pregnant it was the happiest day in both our lives. We decided together that she would quit no later than six months into her pregnancy, and then continue to stay at home to raise our children. That was the normal custom and way of life in the twenties. While it might seem unfair now that women did not pursue lives outside the home, it was not considered a problem then. For good or bad, women bore the children and raised them. Personally, I think all women who spend years caring for children deserve medals for their courage and hard work.

Our first child was born the following year on April 14. Peppinella gave birth to our son, Jiacomo Martino, in the two room flat where we were living. In 1926, medicine was primitive and babies were usually delivered at home by a midwife assisted by a female family member. I was there for the birth, but was shooed away at the critical time. Like all fathers, I paced the floor until I heard the wail of the baby- our first child, and our first son. I can vividly remember my first sight of him. He was a long, tall baby, about six and a half pounds. I was such a proud father and so happy that God had given us a strong healthy baby. There were no words to truly describe my joy at parenthood, my relief at the good health of both my wife and child, and all the dreams I began having for my son. As I held him for the first time, I felt a deep and penetrating love for my new little family.

I'm proud to say that Jack has grown into a successful businessman with his own dental practice. He's a good family man, honest and well-liked by everyone he meets. He's always helping other people and never seems to be able to do enough for me. I like to think Jack inherited his warm, helpful disposition from both Peppinella and me.

Shortly after Jack was born, and just before my twenty-seventh birthday, there was an incredible job opening as head chef at the prominent Brant Inn in Burlington, Ontario, some thirty miles from Toronto. It was a beautiful summer resort hotel. The Inn was open only six months a year, but the understanding was they would pay me well for those six months. I would be in charge of a staff of almost 300! For a man of my age, this was a dream come true. It was such a great opportunity that I couldn't turn it down; I took the job after discussing the pros and cons with Peppinella. She would stay in Toronto living with her mother until the baby was older. I would live at the hotel, commuting to Toronto, until they could join me in a few months. We were saddened by the thought of being separated from one another, but happy for the opportunity this gave me to provide for my family.

The Brant Inn had a grocery store located right on the premises, a large dining room and a room service. They also ran a big dining room out on the waterfront by Lake Ontario. The hotel's restaurant was open from eight o'clock in the morning until two thirty at night. Dances were held in the dining room every night and the place was packed all the time. I was in charge of everything that went on, plus I supervised all special affairs, like banquets and weddings, too. Business was good at the hotel and I must say I felt I had made a real success of myself. For three years, I worked six months at the Brant Inn during the summer, and six months in Toronto during the winter. It was easy for me to find another job for those six months; all my employers knew I was working a summer resort and didn't mind. The bad thing about this arrangement was the commute in order to see my wife and son while I was working at the hotel. I'd travel back and forth once or twice every week to see my family. Once in a while, Peppinella would come back with me to the hotel. I had two rooms in the staff quarters and wives were encouraged to visit or even live there. Because I was the head chef, my accommodations were large and elegant. But with the good always comes the bad, and my hours were extremely long. While Peppinella and I enjoyed being together at the Inn, it wasn't very practical for her to be alone so much.

My life was seemingly perfect. I had a beautiful wife, a healthy son and an exciting job. I was one happy man! In 1928 our second son, Rocco, was delivered into this world. Another strong, handsome boy. We were now blessed with two wonderful children. Peppinella was still coming to visit me at the Brant Inn for a week or two whenever she could. It was a nice break for her, and she could relax and enjoy the lake.

My bubble of happiness, however, was about to burst. When Rocky was eighteen months old, we took him with us to the home of a friend, whose child was near Rocky's age. We thought it might be fun for them to play together. Unknown to any of us at the time, this child had whooping cough and Rocky caught it. It developed into a severe case, one that he fought for several months. His cough had turned into a severe throat infection; the doctor said it was diphtheria. Peppinella and I struggled with agonizing feelings of guilt and stupidity for what happened, but it was no one's fault. God took our second child away from us. Rocky died in my arms gasping for breath. As he died, I prayed to God asking if I could die in his place. But the good Lord saw otherwise. There are no words to truly describe the sorrow, grief, sense of loss and heartache that comes from losing a child. Today, fifty years later, I can still feel the gasp of that poor child struggling to breathe. I was hopeless. No medicine could help him (these were the days before antibiotics and immunization). We really should thank God for the wonders of modern medicine, especially when it comes to saving our children.

For Peppinella, Rocky's death was a mother's special tragedy. Her baby that she nursed to life was gone forever. Both of us grieved, but at least we were there to help one another live through the sorrow. Once again our families were endless sources of strength. Peppinella's brother, Donald, grieving terribly himself, took care of all the funeral arrangements. My brother, Frank, cried with me for days on end. Family members pulled together to help us cope with the shock by taking care of errands and just simply <u>being</u> at our sides. To lose such a bright and beautiful baby, to lose his voice calling "Papa" left me with a deep wound that only time could attempt to heal.

Poor Peppinella. In the middle of her grief she was expecting our third child. Maybe it was a blessing in disguise; planning for a new baby did help to take our minds off our recent loss. The following June we had another son, whom we chose to name "Rocco Leonard". We gave him this name not as a means of replacing his dead brother, but rather as a memorial. My wife once again had the joyful task of raising two children that we could love and care for.

Rocky, like Jack, has grown up to be a wonderful person. He was always a clever, outstanding student and won enough scholarships and prizes in high school to pay his way through University. (It didn't cost me a cent!) He is now a PhD, has four terrific sons, a lovely wife, and a large successful business in the United States that he started on his own. It brings me great joy to know this good man is my son.

To be honest, I always worried about Rocky. He was born such a short time after his brother's death that

I felt both a special closeness and great fear for him. Understandably, Peppinella and I became almost frantic in our efforts to shield him from illness and harm.

I remember a time when I went to look at a house we might buy. I climbed the stairs holding Rocky and suddenly, they gave way. I clutched him as I fell backward and landed with a thump. I was grateful beyond belief...Rocky wasn't harmed. As much as it hurt, I laughed as baby Rocky kept saying "again!" It was the first of many times I thanked God for his protection of Rocky. That special protection seems to have surrounded him all his life.

Rocky was an unusually active child. No matter how much I hovered over him trying to protect him, he just seemed to get himself into trouble. Finally, our worst fears materialized. Just before his second birthday, Rocky fell while playing around the Brant Inn, cutting his leg. Peppinella and I washed it, bandaged it and thought little more of it. Today we probably would have gone to a doctor. In the midst of the Great Depression of the early 30's, not only did we lack a sense of medical need, but we didn't have the extra money. Only if we thought a problem was serious would we seek professional medical help. So, at the time, Rocky's cut didn't seem serious. After a week, his leg still hadn't healed. Peppinella and I finally decided we had to take Rocky to a doctor. The doctor we saw looked at the wound and said it was infected, but thought nothing of it. He told us to bathe it with salt water and apply a poultice twice a day (again, there were no antibiotics). When the wound didn't improve after another week, we took Rocky to a specialist in Hamilton. This doctor looked worried. He told us the leg was badly infected and might have to be amputated. He didn't seem able to offer us any other solution.

I didn't want to have such drastic surgery performed on my son unless it was the only option, so that night the three of us drove to Toronto's Hospital for Sick Children. I asked to see a "Doctor Brown" of whom I had read. Doctor Brown was a kind man and renowned in Canada for his successful work with children. He talked to Rocky as if he were his own child. Despite the pain, Rocky took a liking to Dr. Brown and stopped crying as his leg was examined.

The verdict was good news and bad. Dr. Brown would operate the next day, but wasn't sure if his procedure would work. Apparently Rocky had "osteomyelitis", a severe bone infection just below his right knee. If the operation wasn't successful, the leg would have to be amputated anyway and Rocky's life might be threatened. Before we could blame ourselves though, Dr. Brown kindly made it clear that we had acted properly regarding Rocky's injury. His infection was a rare one, and this doctor wasn't surprised that the one in Hamilton hadn't been too helpful or knowledgeable.

Peppinella and I were worried, of course, but felt that if anyone could save Rocky's leg as well as his life, it would be Dr. Brown. We also had no choice. Dr. Brown arranged for us to stay in the hospital overnight and the next day he operated with good results. Within a day or two, Rocky wanted to go home, but needed to stay in the hospital for a few weeks to make sure the infection was gone. As Rocky grew, the size of the scar gradually decreased in size. Years later when I saw him play football, hockey, and baseball, I thanked the good Lord for sparing his leg.

A near-tragedy struck again when Rocky was five. One day his temperature started to climb for no reason. It reached 106° and nothing Peppinella and I did would lower it. The doctor we took him to despaired, informing us Rocky would be dead the next day. I don't know what the cause of the fever was, but he certainly was sick. Peppinella and I started to panic, but then immediately thought of Rocky's previous crisis. I phoned Toronto. Dr. Brown was away, but a great family friend of ours, Dr. Glionna, was available. We called him and he told us to get Rocky to Toronto by ambulance immediately. Within an hour Rocky and Peppinella were on their way, while I stayed in Hamilton to look after Jack.

Once again God smiled on us. Dr. Glionna's treatments worked and within two days, Rocky's temperature was normal. Dr. Glionna had tried a new medication on him, a forerunner of the miracle sulpha drug of the 30's. It saved his life. Peppinella and I knew Rocky was all right when he wanted his red fire truck (my brother-in-law, Donald, drove to Hamilton to get it). A few days later, I had the chance to join everyone in Hamilton. I cried as I held Rocky, thankful beyond belief for his recovery.

As I mentioned, Rocky seemed to lead a charmed life. He climbed everything in sight- including all the fruit trees in our backyard- and never got hurt. One night I came home and there was Rocky at the top of the telephone pole! He was eight at the time. Trees were just a minor challenge for Rocky, so I guess he felt he had to advance to the next level! Years later as Rocky traveled all over North America and Europe, I learned of other narrow escapes. He was in one plane crash, another airplane struck by lightning, and several cars hit from behind. Somehow, he always came out unscathed. The most serious incident happened shortly after Rocky was married. Returning from a wedding in New York, in an ice storm, his car rolled over three times on the New York Thruway. He only suffered six cracked ribs. To this day, I am certain in my belief that Rocky has received special protection. Maybe God felt it was only fair to protect my second chance at having a second son.

EDITOR'S NOTE: Pop was right! For some reason, I have always felt protected. Situations in my life that could have been very bad just seemed to work out. After Mom died, I felt this sense of protection even more. This struck me once when I was writing some tough exams. I remember panicking, my mind going totally blank and then suddenly feeling all right- the answers started flowing through my head as if someone were telling them to me. I could almost feel my mother's presence. After Pop died, I felt the same kind of presence when things were difficult.

Another time, I came home from the office feeling awful and went straight to bed. I had been taking antibiotics for a chronic ear infection. Suddenly, I felt seriously weak and thought I was going to lose consciousness. Just as suddenly, I sensed strength flowing back. Then the phone rang; it was Pop. He wanted to know if I was all right. He told me how he had felt I was in trouble. At that point, I assured him I was fine. As he hung up, my brother- who rarely phoned- called. He, too, seemed worried, asking if I was all right. This family closeness and caring seemed to envelope my mind and body and in an hour or two, I felt much better. I have since found out I have allergic reactions to some antibiotics; that night I was probably close to anaphylactic shock.

Incidents throughout my life such as these seem to support Pop's belief in special protection. (Perhaps it's my older brother Rocky looking after me).

I loved my boys and loved being with them. I spent as much time as possible with both of them. Jack, however, was a much quieter child than Rocky. Rarely mischievous, he didn't get himself into the accident-type situations that Rocky seemed to be drawn to all the time. Jack also had a friendly, outgoing personality and was a joy to be with. As the first born son, his grandmother and great aunts competed over who could do more for him or feed him the most. One night I saw Peppinella's mother, Annuziata, and her sister, Mary, sitting on either side of Jack feeding him lady finger cookies! To say the least, his weight blossomed until I insisted he stop eating so many cookies and start eating more vegetables. Like me, Jack was not only roly poly, but happy go lucky and content in anything he did. When I went to the park with the boys, Jack always stayed and walked with me, while Rocky jumped over all the rocks. When we went fishing, Jack baited his hook and tried to catch fish, while Rocky got wet. (If he did try to fish, the line usually got caught in his trousers first!) I still enjoy thinking about all those wonderful days.

When Jack was about 5 or 6 years old, I started calling him "Mino", a nickname for Jacomino. It was my private term of endearment for him, so close to "nino", the Italian word for baby. We had a lot of fun at our house on Minto Street. Peppinella and I played often with our children in the big back yard. She increasingly relished her roles of wife and mother as we enjoyed our family life together. It was the only time we were ever really alone in our own home. The house itself had three bedrooms and a big basement where the boys played on rainy days. They were so crazy about airplanes, especially Mino, that they built one out of cardboard boxes in the basement. When I would come home from work at night they made me pretend to be the mechanic, pulling on the propeller while they made loud engine noises.

Our two boys were always "curious", to say the least. Once, Mino wanted to see if a match would go out in an inkwell full of cleaning fluid. Luckily, he tried his experiment in the sink. Rocky liked to climb <u>inside</u> the house, too, especially on chairs. God only knows why, but one time he decided to try standing on top of the back of a chair. Bang! Good thing he had a hard head. It bled for an hour while Peppinella and I frantically rushed him to the hospital. Once again there was no damage- except to our nerves. I suppose all of this was routine in the daily life of two active boys. What else should we have expected? But sometimes, we prayed for a little less activity.

"THE GREAT DEPRESSION"

In 1931, I was faced with economic hardship for the second time. It was the Great Depression of the thirties and certainly reminded me of its 1911 predecessor: unemployment, scarcity of money, melancholy. People in Canada were living on vouchers- a kind of city-sponsored food stamp program. I had left the Brant Inn and was now working as head chef of "Murphy's Restaurant" in Hamilton. There were two locations that I was responsible for, but spent most of my time at a three story building with a delicatessen, restaurant, grill room and banquet hall. Murphy's also had their own bake shop and butchering facilities. The prices of our meals were reasonable, but people just didn't have the extra money to eat at restaurants.

I remember what a sad sight it was when the farmers used to come to the Hamilton Market. Often these poor men couldn't even sell their produce at a loss and would have to take it home with them. People simply didn't have the cash to buy it. Bushel baskets of tomatoes were sold for twenty cents; eggs were twelve cents a dozen; bread was six cents a loaf; and the best grade butter was only fifteen cents a pound. Meat and poultry were also sacrificed at ridiculously low prices. Chickens sold for fifteen cents a pound. Entire lobster or steak dinners went for seventy-five cents. A hotel room for one night, which included a full course dinner, averaged about a dollar.

With these prices, it would seem that people could get by with very little money. Yet most workers' incomes were not large enough to accommodate even the smallest of purchases. My kitchen staff each grossed only ten dollars a week, while they worked twelve hours a day, seven days a week. My cooks earned twenty dollars a week, and my assistant, thirty-five. We all worked the same long, hard hours. As head chef, I was fortunate enough to earn sixty dollars a week. This was an incredible amount of money during the Depression.

Because Murphy's Restaurant had only a minimal profit margin, it was my responsibility to think of ways to boost our business. On nights when the third floor of the building was empty, I would arrange to rent a band and hold a dance. Admission was fifty cents per couple, including juice and sandwiches. On Saturdays, the restaurant would also host a play in the banquet hall with an admission of seventy-five cents. Attendees would frequently go to the dining room afterwards and spend fifteen cents more on pie and coffee. Though there wasn't much money left after we paid for the service and the door prize and the band, the trick was to bring a crowd. These dances and plays never drastically increased profits, but every little bit helped.

Things in general were really tough. It was a scary time. The number of people living on the streets increased dramatically. So did the beggars asking for money so they could buy something to eat. I know this happens even today, but during the Depression, whole families were literally starving. There also weren't the kind of panhandlers who are "professional" or want money strictly for drugs or alcohol. Hungry people often came to my kitchen asking for food. No one, and I mean no one, ever went away from my kitchen hungry or empty-handed. This was true not only throughout the Depression, but in all the years before and since. There is always plenty of food left over in a restaurant at the end of the day, no matter how carefully you plan. In my case, I preferred to give it to those who came and asked rather than throw it away. None of us knows when we might need a helping hand. As my mother taught me, "There but for the grace of God go I."

EDITOR'S NOTE: I witnessed Pop's caring first hand when I worked for him at the restaurant during summer breaks while in high school and college. No one who asked for food ever went away hungry. When I was there, a few came who were truly down and out as I imagine during the Depression. Still and all, he was true to his word. He did what he could to help the hungry and homeless. He gave food, but I also know he often reached into his own pocket for a monetary handout. Throughout his life, Pop never forgot his own humble beginnings. While his family was well above the poverty line, there were no "extras". Hard work was needed to take care of everyone, and to make sure all children were well fed and well clothed. The family always came first. You cared for your own. But you also cared for others because they too were your brother and sister. Pop learned this from his parents as a family tradition. I knew Pop. I wish I had known his parents too.

I suspect that today, there might be more street people evident than in Pop's day, even in the midst of the Depression. Back then, homeless people tended to head for the countryside, because life was easier there than in the city. Now the homeless stay in the city. Today many are derelicts by choice, in a sense, because of their drug addiction or mental problems. It's really a crime that governments have solved some of their budget problems by opening the doors of the mental asylums, and sending more poor souls into the streets.

This shortsighted solution has probably cost more than the kinder and more effective way used in the past. I am sure that Pop would have been very upset to know that government budgets go more for bureaucracy than for a helping hand. However, knowing Pop as I do, I am sure it would have made no difference whatsoever to him. For whatever reason, if someone was hungry, Pop would feed them. If in need of comfort, Pop would do what he could.

Though living through the Depression was difficult and often frustrating, it was also a teacher of tolerance and compromise. We learned more than anything to help each other survive. It was serious business; people had to help one another. It's not like today (the early 80's). I don't consider this a depression or even a recession! Everyone has lots of money. It's simply inflated high times; that's what I would call it. In my opinion, the problem comes from everyone overspending themselves and then having a hard time controlling their finances. People need to learn how to realistically live within their means. They spend too much on credit and then find themselves in debt to such an extent that they can't get out.

EDITOR'S NOTE: Pop was always cautious about overspending. His idea was that one dollar saved equaled two he didn't have to earn. Often with a chuckle he would add, "…and maybe four with today's taxes!" He died in 1982 before the even larger spending binges of the later 80's occurred, which are now causing so much economic indigestion. Pop foresaw much of the frenzy of debt and restructuring that marked the second half of the decade- too bad he wasn't the Treasury Secretary of the nation!

I stayed with Murphy's Restaurant for five years. Peppinella and I were so happy and content in those days. Gradually, I got more time off from work: an afternoon every Wednesday and usually most Sundays. Our happiness was not without difficulty. My wife's mother, Annunziata, was a strong-willed person. Naturally, being a widow, she wanted her daughter available and located close to her. My mother-in-law's phone calls and visits became more frequent and more insistent. Peppinella cried a lot, not knowing who to be loyal to or which way to turn. Neither one of us wanted to go back to Toronto, but if you knew Annunziata, you knew she would move heaven and earth until she got her way.

EDITOR'S NOTE: My grandmother was a dear lady. She had a heart of gold and wanted what she believed was best for everyone in the family. She sure gave my father a hard time because like all mothers, no one was good enough for her daughter. She certainly had a double standard when it came to her three sons versus her son-in-law. Taken all together, she was a kindly lady, but a strong-willed one. She lived until 96, after having a pacemaker implanted at the age of 94, setting some kind of medical record in her day. I remember listening in awe when she used to tell me how she was upset at doctors when she went to see them because they seemed more interested in her longevity than they were in what ailed her. She certainly wasn't a negative personality; if anything, she was a strong, positive one. When she died in 1973, an entire era died with her.

Eventually, I made job inquiries in Toronto. The best offer I could get paid was twenty-five dollars a week, less than half what I was making in Hamilton.

My pride wouldn't let me take such a salary cut, even though we could have survived on that. Unfortunately, things at home didn't improve. In 1933, Peppinella had a miscarriage and didn't recover too quickly. I became alarmed and started thinking that perhaps we could use some help. That's also when Rocky got sick with the high fever and almost died. Taking him to Toronto had saved his life. Peppinella decided she wanted to go home- back to Toronto.

After a lot of soul-searching, I decided that if we were going to move back to Toronto, I'd at least try to fulfill a life-long dream of opening my own delicatessen. While still in Hamilton, I found a location in Toronto and immediately started making preparations. During that summer of 1934, we spent days on end making pickles, pickled beets, mustard pickles and all the other items I felt were needed for my new delicatessen. I gave notice of my resignation at Murphy's. The Murphy brothers did everything they could to keep me: they offered a raise, shorter working hours, or whatever I wanted in order for me to stay. When I explained the reasons for my move, they were kind enough to give me their strongest support and best wishes. They also gave me a month's salary- unheard of in those days- and the promise of excellent references if I ever needed them and a job if I ever returned to Hamilton.

So, we moved to Toronto. I opened my delicatessen and also bought my first house at 936 Delaware Avenue. It was a pleasant single home with four bedrooms…small, but comfortable. Because I had stayed single and worked for so many years before our marriage, I had saved enough money to pay for it in full. And I paid the $3,000 it cost me in cash. This is the way I've always dealt with money situations; I've never purchased anything with borrowed funds. We bought all new furniture, too. The house was lovely. Peppinella was content. Annunziata and her two younger brothers, Jimmy and Frank, came to live with us. I hoped this would boost Peppinella's spirits because of both the company and the help. In reality, this was a mixed blessing. Although my mother-in-law did help my wife, her attitude turned out to be a great problem. She looked upon the house as hers, even though Peppinella and I owned it. Anyway, a few months after we moved in, much to our mutual joy, Peppinella got in the family way again.

That year was a hard one in which to start a business. There I was, all alone, reduced from supervising a staff of hundreds of serving buyers of ten cents worth of this and five cents worth of that. Still, it made me happy that Martino's Delicatessen soon became a favorite in the neighborhood. Unfortunately, money continued to be tight and I couldn't make ends meet. Perhaps I strove too much for quality in such a slow market. Whatever the case, by the spring of 1935, I knew my dream was a bust. My brother, Frank, helped me remove my belongings when I finally shut down the shop. It was a sad day for me. We stored the two main counters in my backyard until I finally broke them up for firewood a few months later. They were constant reminders of my failure to "hack it" as a businessman. Like my father before me, this depression had almost ruined me. I was broke and what was worse, I owed Annunziata a thousand dollars she had loaned me to start the business. I believe she enjoyed reminding me of this debt because she did it on an almost daily basis. It was one of the happiest days of my life when I paid her back at the end of a year. Things were very, very tight indeed.

"LOSING A WIFE"

I wound up taking the job at twenty-five dollars a week that I had found out about before. I became the head chef at the Biltmore Restaurant in the heart of downtown Toronto. The salary was barely enough to support a wife and family, let alone pay back my mother-in-law and take care of Peppinella's medical expenses while she was pregnant. I was even trying to send money home, too, because I knew how difficult things still were for my parents. I suppose I got along all right at the Biltmore. With the exception of the pay, it was a good job, and everyone was friendly. Eventually, I felt right at home (and continued to work for the owner, Mr. Michael P. Georgas, for the next 23 years!)

Peppinella's pregnancy was becoming increasingly difficult for her to tolerate. She would have pain and bleed unexpectedly, so her doctor told her to stay in bed as much as possible. She went to St. Michael's Hospital in Toronto for her delivery this time and gave birth to a baby girl. Our daughter lived for only twenty minutes because she was born premature at seven months. Today, modern medical care could have saved her life. I grieved over the death of my daughter, but Peppinella's poor condition at the time put all other thoughts out of my mind. It was only later that I truly remembered the ache for that beautiful baby girl we never had a chance to love.

Peppinella had hemorrhaged badly during the birth. The doctors' efforts had been tremendous in trying to save her life. She was so weak and had lost so much blood that she remained in the hospital for about three months afterwards. Of course, I made absolutely sure she had a private room and good nurses. I did everything I could for her. Peppinella eventually returned home an invalid in need of constant care. I was told by her doctor that she had about a fifty percent chance of recovering- she had almost died. He doubted if she would even live for another two years. At any rate, she would never fully regain her former health.

Needless to say, this was a time of serious financial distress for me. My wife's medical bills totaled $7,000 and medical insurance didn't yet exist in 1936. The Sisters of St. Joseph nuns who ran the hospital couldn't have been nicer, though. They knew about my predicament and totally ignored their own costs. They were so caring and understanding, telling me to pay whatever and whenever I could. That's just what I did. It took me five long years, but I paid back every cent. They never charged me any interest on my debt, and even shaved some of it down, I'm sure. To this day, I can't fully express my gratitude enough for those wonderful ladies who ran their hospital with love as well as science.

Now I was truly grateful we had moved to Toronto. Peppinella's Aunt Lena, Annunziata's youngest sister, became her constant companion. Lena lived a ten minute walk away and was only ten years older than Peppinella. They treated each other more like sisters than aunt and niece. All of my wife's family helped. In her delicate physical condition, Peppinella needed all the family love and support she could get.

Over the course of the two years before her death, Peppinella suffered serious emergencies on more than one occasion. Her circulation was bad; her breathing was so restricted she constantly gasped for air. During a seizure, in kindness and love, a hot water bottle was placed at her feet. It burned her right foot terribly. For the last five months of her life, she limped whenever she was well enough to walk. Christmas of 1937 was particularly bad. Peppinella was in bed and very, very ill. Right after the New Year arrived, she managed to get up and dressed. I begged her to be careful, but she just laughed in her quiet way and said, "I'll be all right! Let me at least try to be a companion to you for the short time I have left." Peppinella had always been smart and knew what was happening without anyone telling her. We tried to shield her, but she wasn't fooled. My wife faced her illness and imminent death with courage and reason, albeit with sadness. I often noticed the looks she directed at our sons, like she already missed them. Several times I saw tears in her eyes, but then she would regain her composure and smile. I loved her more and more each day. At the same time, I could do less and less for her.

Both of our families continually prayed for Peppinella's health. We hoped against all odds that she would eventually recover, but this wasn't God's plan. On January 25, 1938, my wife died of heart failure. She was only thirty-seven years old. While we all knew it was inevitable, it still came as a great shock.

The night Peppinella died was actually a very beautiful evening. Lena had come over to visit. They both sat in the living room for a long time, laughing a lot and talking over old times. Rocky and Jack were with us, thrilled to see their mother so happy. Around 9:30 p.m., Lena left and I took the boys up to bed. I heard Peppinella coming up the stairs alone before I had a chance to go down and help her. Then I heard a sigh come from our bedroom and a slight thump. I left the boys and rushed down the hall. There was my beloved wife lying on the floor. Her lips were blue-black and her face a ghastly white. I called her name. She smiled at me, and then let out another sigh. I yelled for Annunziata and she raced down to the corner for the doctor. Hearing all the commotion, the boys came in and saw their mother lying there. They started to cry. The doctor arrived immediately, but sadly informed us Peppinella was dead.

Peppinella was a happy, loving woman with incredible patience and a level head. She loved life and was everything I had ever dreamed of in a wife. She was my companion, the mother of my children and my best friend. We had a wonderful, full life before her illness. She and I faced all kinds of tragedy and difficulty together, and somehow she always made it seem bearable with her quiet nod that said, "It'll be all right." All the heartache and sorrow of those tragic moments comes back to me now. Forty years drop away in an instant. Peppinella was a remarkable woman.

It was hard for Jack, Rocky and me to get accustomed to the loss of this good lady, who was so special to all of us and so much a part of our lives. I had an especially hard time coping because I knew I had the responsibilities of a family to contend with. Somehow, I was going to have to force myself to go to work and take care of my boys. Of course, everybody had a lot of advice to give after the funeral. It was a depressing, confusing time. I now prayed to the Lord to give me strength. My children had lost their mother…they couldn't very well afford to lose their father.

As was the custom in those days, for a time after Peppinella died, she lay in a casket in the front room of our home. This is where she stayed right up until the time of her burial. What a sight. On the day of her funeral, the street was full of people. Everyone was especially sad because she had died so young. She was well liked, too. She had never bothered or offended anybody. Mourners came from all over to attend the funeral. Our families arranged for a Mass Service to be held at a church at Grace and Dundas Streets. The funeral ceremony was lovely, the best I could afford. I made sure my Peppinella was buried in a nice plot, too. Despite the ceremony and the ritual, it didn't change the fact that my wife was dead. It didn't take away my sadness or my sense of loss. What was I going to do? How would I keep myself going?

While Peppinella had been lying in the coffin at home, I took an oath to her. I silently promised her that I would never leave the boys so long as I was in the world. At least until they got married, I would not leave them. While they were in my care, I would make sure they got the best I could give. With the help of God, I succeeded in keeping that promise. Today I am proud of my sons and how they grew up. They both stand on their own feet and don't depend on anyone. They're married with wonderful families. They're good, productive citizens. Maybe losing their mother at a young age helped make them so self-reliant. What a terrible price to pay for character!

CHAPTER SIX

THE MIDDLE YEARS
"RAISING SONS ALONE"

I was now left alone to raise my sons Jack, who was eleven, and Rocky, who was eight. Despite their young ages when Peppinella died, they always did a lot around the house to help. Every day, Rocky used to make breakfast and wash the dishes, while Jack would sweep the floors, make the beds, and straighten the house. I always felt it was their strength and God's will that enabled me to survive- to pick up the pieces of my life and go on living. Those years I spent raising and teaching my children were probably the years I learned the most as well. They taught me how to be strong, caring, and determine what was really important in life during this difficult time.

How was I going to take care of two boys when I was working seventy hours or more a week? How would I manage without a wife? I just didn't have the extra time to take care of all the household chores and feed and care for my sons. I had the job of being not only a father but a mother to Rocky and Jack. Plus, I had my own grief, which at times seemed unbearable. My brother, Frank, and my sister, Angelina, were

143

endless sources of strength and understanding. Annunziata, who was undoubtedly suffering terribly and perhaps even blaming me for her daughter's death, was no help. In fact, she made things so much worse with her constant criticizing and complaining that I finally had to ask her to leave after about six months. She did. I was left in a four bedroom house alone with two children. My wife's Aunt Lena became a godsend, however. She kindly agreed to take the boys in every day to feed them and do their laundry until I could work out some kind of arrangement.

Of course, I thought about remarrying right away, but really didn't have my heart in it. It would have only been a marriage made out of convenience, attempting to replace a mother for Jack and Rocky. I didn't want to do that. It wasn't right. It wouldn't have been fair to the woman, the boys, or me. Friends suggested I put my children in boarding school. That was easier said than done. I had no money and I refused to part with my sons. Aside from my sincere vow to Peppinella, to institutionalize young lads for my own convenience was also not right. I rejected that idea without a second thought. My wife's aunts did offer to care for Jack but no one wanted Rocky. I think he was too rambunctious and adventurous for them- a real "handful". Naturally, Jack, being so polite and well-disciplined, was everyone's darling. Once again I rejected their offers. No one would take either of my boys. I decided it was my problem and I would solve it. That time seems so distant now. Both my sons turned out to be happy, successful family men, so I guess I made the right decision. It was a tough choice, but we survived.

For the most part, things went smoothly for us this way. I would always pick up Rocky and Jack at Lena's every night after work. I stayed home every night with them, too. They studied. I helped them with their homework. We played games. In the summertime, we went outside and played baseball. They studied. I was not only their "Pop" but their chum. However, I needed a longer term solution for raising my boys. I thought of my little sister, Maria, back in Italy. She would be nineteen now, so I wrote to my parents asking them if they would finally consider moving to Canada and bringing my sister along to take care of the children. I was elated at their reply. Yes! They would come! I felt like dancing with joy. My greatest hope was going to be fulfilled at last- the rest of my family was coming to America.

It was my job to make all the travel arrangements and start the necessary paperwork for my family to emigrate to Canada. The months passed swiftly, but progress on the paperwork went slowly. Suddenly, there was a problem. Any person applying for immigration status was required to have a physical and Mama's chest x-ray in six months showed a shadow on her right lung. Papa was fine and of course, so was Maria. No matter what guarantees I gave the Immigration Bureau, Mama was not allowed to get her visa until she had another chest x-ray in six months. Papa, however, insisted Maria come alone. With my heart full of sadness and worry, I changed the travel reservations for my family and rebooked Mama and Papa for passage later that year.

Mary (as we called Maria in America) sailed from Naples on the Rotterdam on June 10, 1939. My brother Michael and I went to New York to meet her.

As we waited for Mary's arrival, all I kept remembering was the little four year old girl I had last seen on my visit to Modugno in 1923. All throughout that trip, Mary followed me around like a puppy with the teddy bear I had given her. It was strange and not just a little surprising to see a very sophisticated nineteen year old young woman walk off the ship. And yet, her arrival brought back a lot of memories for me and Michael both since she looked so much like Mama.

The train trip to Toronto was full of reminiscences as Mary brought us up to date on what had happened in Modugno over the last few years. We also talked excitedly about the expected arrival of our parents and how wonderful it would be to have everyone all together again.

When we arrived at my house, Mary made a big fuss over Jack and Rocky. In normal adolescent boy fashion, they were shy and not too sure how to take their young aunt.

The next morning, Sunday, my Uncle Tony came over to visit. We were all enjoying breakfast and he asked Mary how she liked America. All at once, everyone burst out laughing. This was her first day in Toronto and she hadn't even seen the city yet, much less the country, and Tony was asking her how she liked America. One thing Mary did comment on was eating corn flakes for the first time in her life. At first, she wasn't too sure what they were. In fact, she had asked me in Italian if they were dried potato skins. The boys couldn't understand why I was laughing so hard. When I explained, they got a big chuckle out of it too. From that point on, all of us made a real effort not to speak Italian in the house so Mary could learn to speak English. Once she was comfortable with her new language, we relented and she started teaching the boys Italian.

Early on, Jack and Rocky both wanted bicycles, but I said no. I figured that if they had bicycles, they'd be out all the time getting into trouble. I explained to them how when I was young, I had a bicycle and nearly went out of my mind riding it. I told my kids I almost got killed with it, too. They were upset and thought I was the biggest ogre in the world for not letting them have bikes but I was tough. It really bothered me denying them something they wanted so badly, but I truly believed I was doing a good thing. I protected them from all danger whenever I could.

I did allow my boys to go "skating", though. Jack had made two scooters out of lumber scraps and old roller skates for him and Rocky to ride on. They used to love zooming up and down the street. To this day, I still think kids appreciate homemade things more. Now parents buy all kinds of fancy things that their children either don't appreciate or get bored with. It seems like if parents don't produce these fancy gifts, they're convinced they won't get love. I gave my sons shelter, education, and good food. They had a clean home, nice clothes and most importantly, someone to count on- me. I just never bought them extravagant things. Cars and bicycles and such don't mix with studies…especially cars. The first thing you know, it's goodbye homework and hello girlfriends. Just to prove my point, I went without a car myself. I told Jack and Rocky they could have a car when they bought their own.

During most of the time I worked in the Biltmore, my boys were going to school. Jack was fifteen and getting big. He didn't have school on

Saturdays, so I told him he had to come work at the restaurant with me. That's how you make adults of boys- get them started working young. Never give them too many holidays. So I took Jack down to the Biltmore and he started running the dishwashing machine on Saturdays. He was paid two dollars for twelve hours work. Also, I told him he had to buy things he needed with that money; it wasn't to be spent foolishly. Jack kept at his dishwashing job and eventually became my helper in the summertime working with me on the stove. Rocky later started as a busboy at the restaurant when he was fourteen. They worked hard and were tired on Sunday. But on Sunday, of course, I made them go to Church in the morning and Sunday school in the afternoon. My boys were not only going to be educated but they had to learn the laws of God as well. I was determined they were going to grow up to be responsible, hardworking, moral men.

It saddens me to see so many kids today- boys and girls- without any direction in their lives. Having fun seems to be not only the thing at the top of their list, but the only thing on their list! Parties, dancing, running around and growing up just don't mix too well. I've always believed work and discipline were important keys to success in life, and these youngsters don't really understand how valuable this is. I suppose that's another reason why I was so concerned about Jack and Rocky starting work at a young age. I felt obligated to start them off in the right direction.

Of course, it's better to be an educated man. I never forced my boys to study, though I told them it was their decision. They had a choice. Either they could train as chefs and work in the kitchen with me or they could get a good education and do something different.

Whatever they chose, I'd support them. You can't push your child into doing things just because you want them to. Kids have to want it for themselves. You know, you can lead a horse to water, but you can't make him drink. The same goes with people. You can't tell anyone what to do. I've always found that no matter who I'm dealing with- family, friends, and coworkers- allowing other people to have a choice works every time. It's only being fair, really. Everyone is responsible for determining the direction of their own lives.

"ANOTHER WAR"

I always thought Hitler was a madman. Allowing him to succeed in the Second World War would jeopardize everything I believed in. While Italy under Mussolini sided with Hitler in 1940, most Italians, like myself, were strongly anti-Fascist and believed that Mussolini was nothing more than an opportunist. His actions shamed Italy. I could see no good coming from any of it! And nothing did- not in Toronto or the world.

EDITOR'S NOTE: The war years were tough. Pop was concerned about our extended family. We had nephews in the army and my brother was coming up on military age. His own brothers were involved and his younger brother, Ralph, had been in the Italian Army, captured, and then began serving with the British 8th Army. What news did come through wasn't always good. Pop heard of the death of his mother and of his father and it was very difficult for him to accept the fact that he could not be with them or even see them when they died.

Canada during the war years was difficult but not so terrible. We had rationing, but it wasn't very onerous since we never managed to use all of the coupons. We had victory gardens, of course, but even that was no great problem. For me, growing up as a "boy soldier" was interesting because it was a distant war until I started hearing of classmates older than I who had either died in combat or in flying accidents while in training. Then it all became real.

I think for Pop warfare was the ultimate stupidity. That is why I don't think he dictated much about it, because while he lived through it, he really thought it was an absolute waste. He hated war, but that didn't make him a peacenik. If anyone attacked his home or his family, then Pop would be ultra-strong in the defense of those he loved. He couldn't quite understand the wholesale slaughter associated with World War II. For him, it was the second one and after having lived through the first and the flu epidemic, the absurdity of the second war was really beyond him.

As previously mentioned, my brother Frank was put out of business because of World War II. He had a successful grocery store on the main East-West street in Toronto- Blood Street, where it became the Danforth Road. Immediately after the declaration of war, his store front was smashed from people throwing bricks through the windows. Of course, he was terribly insulted and upset. Even worse, pickets paraded outside of his store telling everyone to beware of the "Damned Dago". Within a few weeks of all this, Frank was out of business, seeking work wherever he could get it. Such senseless stupidity! Valueless bigotry! I was more fortunate. At the time, I worked for Michael Georgas, a Greek. He assured me he felt we were both Canadians and that the fight in Europe had no bearing on our relationship. I admired him for that.

At school however, Jack and Rocky ran into some trouble with taunting and name calling. Fortunately, this took place in June of 1940, and school soon ended for the summer. By the fall, things had quieted down considerably as it became apparent many Italians were strongly opposed to Mussolini's action. Italian combat units often refused to fight on the German side and all the way through the war until Italy's surrender in 1943, Italian soldiers were not prominent in fighting on behalf of Hitler. My own brother, Ralph, escaped from a German controlled Italian unit and welcomed service afterwards in the British Eighth Army.

War is strange. My nephew was serving in the Canadian Army; my son, Jack, was in the Canadian Army Dental Corps; my brother was fighting in the British Eighth Army against the Germans, and my brother Frank was put out of business because he was a "damn dago". This kind of nonsensical injustice hurt. It was all so stupid! Thank God sanity eventually prevailed. Italians became more and more accepted as the war progressed, and after the war there was a deluge of Italian immigrants into Toronto- Italians who became an important economic force. Today, I'm proud to assert my Italian heritage, even though I am a Canadian by choice.

The war created some shortages of people in Canada, but really no other major problems. Like the United States, Canada was blessed and spared most of the trauma and misery that accompanies war. The war years happened to be an important growing up time for the boys. Jack finished high school and entered dental college. Rocky started high school and won several impressive scholarships. Both boys were able to attend the private Catholic school in Toronto because tuition was so low and because the boys contributed with their own work during vacation time and with extra money from scholarships. By this time, I was also out of debt. I celebrated this major accomplishment by buying an easy chair, on time. It cost me $50, and I had one year to pay for it. It was the first time I bought something on credit. I sure felt I earned that chair.

The war years passed slowly. Every day brought news that was terrible yet hopeful. We were winning, beating back the threat to decency and life masquerading as Nazism. The cost to the young was terrible. While we bore our share of wounds, thank God we had no wartime deaths in our family.

We weren't really touched on the home front. More and more young people were in uniform, and we had rationing, but it really wasn't burdensome. We always had more than enough, and that gave me a feeling of guilt when I thought of all those poor people who were suffering so much.

I felt the tragedy of war very personally when I learned of my mother's death, and later of my father's. Word came to us through the Red Cross and through members of our family in uniform who were able to check for me. Mother died in 1943, and Papa in 1944. I can't tell you the anguish I felt at learning of their deaths months after the fact. Years later, when I visited Modugno in 1957, I visited both their grave sites and relived those sad moments in the war years when we were all so far apart and without communication.

I can't tell you how much I felt pure joy at the end of the war. We were sure the war would be over early in May of 1945. On Saturday, May 5, I attended the annual inspection parade of the De La Salle Cadet Corps. Rocky, as a high school junior, was only 15 then, and he directed a display of the Signal Corps of the Battalion. His company won the award, and he beamed with pride. I was torn by the contrast with the happiness of these young men with the thoughts that thank God the war was ending or many of the young men on parade that night would die. On Monday, we heard of the Armistice, followed by V-D Day on Tuesday, May 8, 1945.

President Kennedy used to like to say that no one ever said that life was fair. He certainly suffered, and his family suffered, but he always was upbeat and kept working hard for what he thought was right. The war years brought out the best and the worst in people. While I was never directly affected except for some slight prejudices, others suffered, some greatly. My brother, Frank, was put out of business because he was Italian; the Japanese were uprooted from their homes and put into camps because they were Japanese; and Jews were slaughtered in death camps because they were Jews. These people did nothing wrong except to be born what they were. Thank God our world has changed. Maybe we have learned something from the tragedy of war, and that is how to be more human.

War brings out the best, too. I remember the thrill at meeting war veterans, and in particular, one man who graduated from the school my sons attended. He lost both legs in saving others on the battle front. For his bravery, he was awarded the Victoria Cross, the highest honor possible for a Canadian, equal to the Congressional Medal of Honor in the United States. This young man spoke to the students of love for his fellow man, and how he could not stand by and see them killed when he could do something to save them. It is men like him who lessen to some minor extent the total tragedy of war.

We weren't morose during the war. We had some very humorous moments. The funniest sight that I remember to this day was my son Jack. There was a release program for senior high school students to work on farms instead of writing final exams if their grades were high enough. To this day, I laugh uproariously inwardly at the memory of Jack in a straw hat, smelling so high of manure that we couldn't get within ten feet of him. He took a bus to get home each night. He told us he never had a problem getting a seat. Also, the flies never bothered him.

Rocky tried a Victory Garden but he could only grow tomatoes and carrots. Thank God because he loved them. His attempts at pumpkins were an abject failure. I told him it was too much science and not enough labor. I regaled him with stories of my own agricultural pursuits as a young man. When he suggested I help rather than advise, I had a hard time convincing him that my back was too sore to hoe because I had lifted him as a baby and was now old.

Mary, of course, felt the strain more. It was her friends who were being killed. Some of the young men she knew before coming to Canada died in the war, fighting on both sides. This was just another example of the absurdity and stupidity of war mixed with so much personal tragedy.

And so the war years passed in the warmth and love of our family. The tragedies all around us brought us even closer together.

It had been a long war. And like all wars, stupid!

But I'm getting ahead of myself.

It is said that for every cloud there's a silver lining. With tragedy and misfortune behind me, I was certainly due for my share of sunshine. Sure enough, it came towards the end of the war.

"STARTING OVER"

1944 seemed to mark the start of good fortune for me again. This was also the year I was reunited with my childhood friend, Mauro Romita. The feast of St. Rocco on August 16th is a traditional Italian festival. It consisted of a parade with the statue of St. Rocco, bands, a picnic, and a lot of good fun. We always celebrated this holiday or feast on a Sunday so people could come without losing time at work. St. Rocco, or "Santo Rock", in 1944 was a particularly happy feast since we saw the end of the war coming. Many of my fellow immigrants and their children, together with mine, were there to give homage to a great saint, and to have a great time together.

While the procession paraded down the street outside Our Lady of Mount Carmel Church where our Italian feasts centered, I happened to look across the street to the crowd on the other side and immediately saw someone who looked familiar. After a moment I said "Mauro". He was older and bald, but the last time I saw him his head had been shaved so he didn't look much different thirty years later. I started to run towards him shouting "Mauro!" He gave a quizzical look, and then smiled as he, too, started to run towards me. We embraced, laughing and crying with excitement and joy. Here was my best friend from Italy! I couldn't believe it. Though we hadn't seen each other for many years, we were just as comfortable with each other as always.

Mauro, who had been my childhood partner in truancy, had developed into quite a distinguished gentleman. He had left Italy in 1916, just about two years after my departure. He later started the "Castle Ice Company" in New York City, which eventually became the Castle Coal and Oil Company that continues to prosper today. He had also been inducted as a member of the Sovereign Military Order of Malta. The Knights of Malta have been in existence since 1099, originally to defend Christendom. Knights of the Order of Malta are committed to devoting their energies to spiritual and charitable work, particularly with the sick and poor. An influential man in American politics, Mauro further held the position of Chairman of the Democratic Party in the Bronx in New York during the forties and fifties.

Mauro and I picked up as if the thirty year gap had never occurred. He was in New York and I was in Toronto, and even in those days when travel was difficult, we managed to get together two or three times a year, and certainly spent a lot of time on the telephone. We relived all of our youthful experiences, and compared notes on raising children. He had a daughter and four sons, whereas I had Jack and Rocky. The children, too, became great friends and continued the tradition that Mauro and I had established of being close friends within a larger family group.

Mauro was very active in politics and in the church. He was Chairman of the Columbus Day Parade in New York on more than one occasion. In 1949 it was my privilege to be on the reviewing platform with him. Present that day were Governor Averill Harriman and Mayor Robert Wagner. Mauro's friendship was certainly a high point in my life, until his untimely death in 1965. Just before he died, we spoke at length about grandchildren, of whom he had quite a few and I at that time had only two. I continued my association with his family, and with his widow Libertia, but without Mauro it just wasn't the same. I truly miss him and as I write these memoirs, it again brings back his smile and the way he had of saying "ming goog"- the affectionate nickname for those called "Dominic".

After fifteen years of working at the Biltmore, the owner, Mr. Georgas, sold it to begin planning a prestigious new restaurant in Toronto to be named the "Silver Rail". Mr. Georgas asked me to leave the Biltmore and continue my employment for him at the Silver Rail as head chef. It was a wonderful place to be associated with. It had a large, brand new kitchen with a steam cookery, big ovens and a separate butcher department, short order section, service department and bake shop. The restaurant opened to an immediate success. I had spent five months working hard to get everything ready for the Grand Opening. We served two thousand meals that first day and the line waiting to get in stretched around the block. We fed a lot of people there everyday. Around Christmas time, the number could reach as high as three thousand. The Province of Ontario had also just changed the law so it was now legal for restaurants to serve alcohol. Naturally, the bars upstairs were always busy, too. This was my best job yet. I loved it!

I thoroughly enjoyed working for Mr. Georgas. He let me run the restaurant just like it was my own. I managed all the money, ordered the liquor and food, and paid the employees. He and I spoke the same "language", since we had been together for so many years, and in a few minutes we could agree on many decisions. Some people thought he was a hard man to get along with, but he was just demanding. I never had any trouble with him; we never had an argument in all the time I knew him. I think he was a perfectionist like I was. I always did my work promptly and correctly. We must have made a good team, because the Silver Rail restaurant was consistently given excellent reviews, not only for our food, but as a successful business. Working there actually made me kind of famous!

During my stays at the Silver Rail, we catered often for City Hall. Being the head chef, I was in charge of many different events. The most important one was the yearly afternoon tea for three hundred and fifty city employees. I would personally supervise everything-from setting up tables to arranging flowers and decorations. Lots of well-known people were invited and it was a good way for me to get to know important citizens of Toronto. The tea was always held after the city elections took place.

One of the really enjoyable things that happened as a result of all this publicity and exposure was that the editors of *Canadian Hotel and Restaurant* magazine approached me to do a monthly column for them. I offered cooking tips to my fellow chefs, suggested new recipes, and generally wrote about food preparation and trends in the industry. Sometimes, writing a column every month was a chore, but I took it very seriously. I knew that with all my experience I had something valuable to offer the magazine's readers. I must have done a good job because by 1952, McLean-Hunter Publishers (who owned *Canadian Hotel and Restaurant*) asked me to compile all my columns and edit them for incorporation into a book. I ended up writing two, *Recipes for Chefs* and *More Recipes for Chefs*. Writing wasn't exactly my favorite thing to do, so I turned down their offer to publish a third. Well, at least I made my contribution to cooking posterity!

About the same time I started writing my magazine column, I had begun entering various cooking competitions. I won several prizes, usually "First" in my chosen category and on two occasions, "First" overall. I enjoyed it, of course, but the pressure was tough to take at times. The categories at these shows usually included: Pastries, Desserts, Sculptures, Roasts, Fish, Bread and Rolls, Appetizers and Salads. There were basically three placings you could win in each class: the Grand Prize (First), Second and Third, along with Honorable Mention. There was also Best in Show Award winners. Awards at these cooking shows were highly coveted. For some establishments, it could mean substantial increases in business. For the preparers, it could mean money, better jobs and increased recognition. Because of this, the restaurants always produced wonderfully decorated, elaborate displays. Everything was perfect and made to impress. Food was presented in such creative ways you can hardly imagine! However, in the final analysis, taste ruled. If it didn't taste right, it didn't matter <u>how</u> pretty it was.

It was during this time that I also enjoyed the privilege and distinction of being elected to the Epicurean Circle of London as a Master Chef. This is the highest and most prestigious honor that can be bestowed on anyone in the culinary trade. As a Master Chef of Canada, I had the added honor of being one of the senior judges at the annual cooking show held by the Canadian Restaurant Association. This show was held every spring and drew thousands of people. I was part of a panel chosen from all over Canada that consisted of food columnists, food managers and professional chefs, such as me. Naturally, being a judge excluded me from entering as a competitor. In fact, I no longer felt it was fair for me to enter any competitions, so I gave it up to insure my reputation for impartiality. I regretted doing this, but it was a small sacrifice to make to enjoy the privilege of judging.

Being a sincerely honest man, during the twelve years I served as a judge, I felt great responsibility to be objective and fair. For example, some chefs have a special way of crimping or marking pies that is almost a signature. If I even slightly suspected I knew who had baked or prepared a dish, I excused myself from judging that entry. I had to be sure my opinion was absolutely impartial. Maybe that's why I lasted so long as a judge.

In the process of judging food, I always looked for three important features: sight, aroma and taste. My approach was to use the entry's appearance as the first stage of selection. I would walk up to the display table, stand back and sweep all the items with my eyes. I looked for what stood out- arrangement, color, sharpness or creativity. This phase usually eliminated a third to a half of the field from further judging. My next step was to determine aroma. I sniffed each entry carefully, seeking to detect aromas that were pleasing, fresh and not overpowering. Those I found satisfactory were selected for final judging. Eye appeal and aroma had to make me want to taste the item. Of course taste (except for sculptures) was the ultimate test. Taste requirements varied according to the specific food. Combinations of flavors could make or break a dish, however. The right amount of mustard, the right kind of sauce (or absence of one), or the right touch of mint would all make a difference in my decision. For desserts, true flavor not masked by sweetness or tartness was essential. For roasts, fish, and poultry, taste had to be firm, yet not overbearing. Like an artist, I would try and put myself into the mind of the chef, striving to sense what he or she was attempting to achieve. There is a magic to fine food. Year after year the same master chefs seemed to win in one or more categories. Of course, it was always satisfying to see a new young chef start showing at the level of Honorable Mention and work his way up to a Blue Ribbon. We judges enjoyed sharing the happiness of a new champion. That's the part I miss most from my professional days as a chef and judge. After twelve years, I was asked many times to return to judging, but I never felt it would be fair to competitors. With my failing eyesight, I couldn't do them justice. Besides, there were many younger men and women who wanted the opportunity to judge.

As a boy of thirteen, I had set a goal for myself- a goal that I knew could only be achieved through hard work, perseverance and a little bit of luck. At last as a Master Chef, I was filled with a sense of fulfillment and pride, for I had succeeded in making my dream a reality. In the world of cooking, I was recognized as one of the best.

It was the late 40's and almost ten years had passed since Peppinella died. My children and my work were my whole existence, but there was an empty part of my life that only a woman could fill. I hadn't gotten married right after my wife died, though. I did try dating a few times. Once, while I was working at the Biltmore, I dated a nice-looking widow. I was about forty at the time; she was a bit younger and we both had two children. Our friends kept telling us what a nice couple we made. I did enjoy her company, but was afraid that starting a marriage with four children was a dangerous move. After several years alone, I just wasn't ready for both a new wife <u>and</u> a family! We were also young enough and capable of having more children. This wasn't what I wanted. Despite my reservations, my brother talked me into inviting her and her children over for a family dinner so our kids could meet. She accepted the invitation. Dinner went smoothly enough and we all had a pleasant time. Suddenly, we heard squabbling among the children playing in the living room. Who was doing the squabbling? My kids and hers. The other children who happened to be there had stayed out of it. Needless to say, that ended any serious thoughts I had of marrying her. I wasn't about to get myself into a situation with divided camps- her two against my two.

I just wanted to meet someone who was single with no children. Unfortunately, it seemed like those I was attracted to who were single didn't want me because I had children, and those who liked me had children. So, I took my time and waited until I found the kind of woman I was looking for. At last, I was introduced to Pietrina Beatrice Barone at a party. Bea was a kind, lovely woman and we dated throughout the winter and spring of 1948 and were engaged by the following summer. On October 11, 1948, we became man and wife. Our wedding reception was a beautiful feast held at the Silver Rail.

Getting married a second time leads to many mixed emotions. It is nothing like the first love, especially when it results in such wonderful children. I didn't feel any guilt at remarrying, but I did feel a sense of sadness because, despite the joy of the occasion, it did recall my first marriage to Peppinella in April of 1925. Somehow or other I felt that Josephine knew and approved, especially since I had waited until the boys were grown before remarrying.

Bea and I got along fine; we were married for twenty-seven years. She had waited to marry for a long time, too, because she was the head of a big family. We were both very similar in our personalities...family was of great importance to us. Bea's parents had lots of children and her father could never make enough money to support them all, so she worked for years as a sample maker at an embroidery machine. She made a good salary and spent it educating her sisters and brothers. Bea was like a mother to them as I was like a father to mine. If nothing else, we had our great love of family in common.

Our life together was quiet. After all, we were both so close to 50 when we got married. These were quiet years and we both enjoyed a strong bond of family on both sides.

Bea had a way with plants that was unbelievable. She turned her house into a garden, both inside and out. At one time, I thought this was overdoing it, but I rapidly changed my mind when I realized the skill that it took and the beauty that it created. After she died in 1975, I did what I could to keep the plants alive. Needless to say, I missed her "green thumb".

Bea's companionship helped me a great deal through my illnesses as I began to sense my own mortality and as I encountered illness.

She was a very special help in working on the various recipes as I prepared them, quite often joshing me in the process. In the early years of our marriage, I was still a master chef at the Silver Rail. As I will detail later, I retired in the mid 1950's and after that, devoted myself to doing odd jobs around the house, in writing, and in working with my son Jack.

To sum it all up, our life together was quite similar as that of any long-married couple after the children are grown. In our case, while they were not her children, they were both grown and it was really a case of the two of us living in quiet harmony together.

I have always enjoyed spending time with children. They all desire deeply to be loved and seem to naturally want to please the adults that they're with. I suppose raising my sons myself also made me more sensitive and appreciative of their wants and needs. About the time I married Bea and no longer had children of my own to care for at home, I decided to get involved in helping some of the pediatric surgery patients at Toronto's Hospital for Sick Children. A friend of mine had a sixteen millimeter projector, and every Friday night we rented a movie and played it for the kids at the hospital. This was in 1948- long before closed-circuit television, game rooms and the kind of cheery casual children's units they have today. These kids were by themselves in rooms with ominous looking equipment. They were scared and lonely, and my heart bled for them. They were so grateful for any amount of attention they got. Even small doses of fun went a long way in helping them to feel normal again.

EDITOR'S NOTE: These movies Pop played leaned heavily towards Tarzan, talking mules, and talking donkeys. Of course, there were also the requisite shoot-em-up westerns. Ronald Reagan managed to show up in most of these movies. I wonder if any of those children could have possibly known they were watching a future president!

Anyway, it was a great way for me to spend Friday evenings. Rocky would often come, too, to help wheel all the boys and girls into a special area for the movie. Many of them had to be carried, body casts and all, from their beds to stretchers and then back to beds in the movie area. I made sure we ran those movies every week for fourteen weeks, no matter what happened. Even during Hurricane Hazel in 1954, I made sure I was there. The storm was pretty frightening; the wind was terrible. It was the only hurricane ever to hit Toronto, but I couldn't disappoint those sick kids.

Starting in 1950 I also started hosting parties at the Hospital for Incurable Children. Needless to say, these children were terribly sick and often had only a short time to live. It was heart rending for me to see them smile in their pain and suffering. One girl in particular remains in my memory after almost forty years. I think her name was Betty. She was thirteen years old and had fatal kidney disease. She knew she would die in a few months, and all she wanted was to dress as a bride. This young woman knew she'd never get the chance to marry. I gave her a very special party- a costume party. She did dress as a bride, and she looked absolutely beautiful. I baked a special cake and decorated it. To this day, I remember with tears in my eyes the sorrow I felt at such a devastating illness for one so young. Of course, we must never be maudlin at parties; we have to smile and laugh and try and make it memorable for those who are ill. But it is tough smiling when you feel such a heavy leaden weight in your heart. Now, of course, with dialysis she would have had a chance at life.

There were many other incurably sick children at that party. We did our best to make them forget, even for a few moments, the difficulties they faced. We knew then, and I know now, that many of them died at a very young age. Despite their illnesses, they were all full of joy, very realistic, and kids like all the others. While we certainly gave of ourselves, we received infinitely more in return. The vitality and good nature of these incurably sick children, many of them facing death, gave us a sense of hope that if they could accept what fate had given them, then we, too, could accept whatever fate dealt us.

I continued the movies and parties for as many years as my health and time constraints would allow. I loved doing it. The kids all seemed to get so much joy out of my visits! Just knowing I had made even a dent in their despair made me feel wonderful and needed. If possible, I would never have stopped. My only regret was that the long hours of my various jobs in the past had kept me from starting sooner.

CHAPTER SEVEN

THE REFLECTIVE YEARS
"BEING A GRANDFATHER"

I always loved being around children, but I relished being a father to my sons. Parenting was the most rewarding job I ever had. It's so satisfying to know that you're responsible for contributing honest, hard-working, loving human beings to this planet- that you've "made a difference" in the world. When you come to be a grandfather, this feeling grows even stronger and becomes more of an unrestricted joy. I know how I feel when my grandchildren come to visit. My house lights up. Me eyes open up and I become more aware. I feel so good. It's wonderful to be alive and watch my grandchildren growing up, knowing they're truly a part of me. My grandsons and granddaughter are all smart and caring individuals who make me proud. Among my grandchildren, I must count my sister Maria's two girls, Donna and Joanne. Both are as precious to me as my own grandchildren. Maria is like a daughter to me. I love her so much for helping raise my boys, and for being such a companion to me over so many years. I love to phone her and pass the time of day, often many times a day, and certainly

167

for more than a few moments. Especially now as I dictate this, I remember so many good times with her and her two girls.

I feel that all my grandchildren help motivate me to stay alive. There's so much I want to teach them and show them so their lives might be easier. Of course, I also pray to God to keep them growing up in the right direction. I often think about their real grandmother, too, and it hurts me that Josephine isn't around to love them with me. I know she would want to spend lots of time with our grandchildren and have plenty of advice of her own to offer them.

I can still remember my first grandchild as she entered our lives. Josephine Anne, or JoAnne as we called her, was a great joy to my son Jack and his wife Betty, and to Bea and me. She changed a great deal of our lives because once again, we had a young one around. In 1959, I sold our home on Oriole Parkway and moved to DeVere Gardens in Toronto across the street from Jack. Hence, I had plenty of opportunity to see JoAnne grow up, watching her learn to skate on the rink that Jack built on the lawn, and seeing her going to school.

All through her growing years, JoAnne would drop in periodically, like a breath of fresh air, coming to visit Nana and Grandpa.

It wasn't the same with Rocky's sons, as they were born beginning in 1963. I talked to them on the telephone and saw them periodically, but it wasn't the same as being across the street.

My second grandchild was a boy, Peter Dominic, named after me. I was so happy when Rocky called me. The distance melted with the news. Shortly after that, we went to New York for the Christening and

I saw my first grandson. He was followed by three brothers during the next ten years. Whenever I was with them, in Toronto, in Philadelphia, or at Rocky's summer home on the ocean, I felt an unbelievable sense of joy. While my heart ached at not seeing them that often, still I was so happy to be with them. Jo Anne, living across the street, filled the void of not being with all my grandchildren all the time.

Rocky often called me for advice on how to handle the boys. They were as "alive" as he had been. I remember how I always counseled patience. I reminded him that a prime stallion must be taught to be ridden, and must never be broken. I know he took my lessons to heart because his four boys are a joy to all of us.

I hope this doesn't sound like a slight to my granddaughter. I love all five of my grandchildren infinitely, equally. With Rocky's four boys, however, since I only saw them two or three times a year, those occasions stand out in my memory very strongly.

Jo Anne's wedding was a particularly happy time for me. It was on August 9, 1980. All five of my grandchildren were there, and all my living friends. I was 80 and danced the Charleston that night, even if a little slower than I did sixty years ago.

We all see ourselves in our grandchildren. By their very presence, we know that the family will continue. The surname is not as important as the continuity. If Rocky's children had been girls, it would still be the name. Boys or girls, grandchildren are all equal, precious, and vital to the family. God love and bless them all!

EDITOR'S NOTE: Pop was always great with my four sons. While their visits with him either in Toronto or Philadelphia were relatively infrequent, they were always lengthy, giving the boys the chance to get to know him. If they weren't helping him dictate his reminiscences, they usually tried to take him sailing. The wise man that he was, Pop more often than not happily chose sailing with them over dictation. He knew how important their sport was to them and it was just as important to Pop to share in their excitement and joy. My sons always loved talking to him if they couldn't be with him. Thank God for the phone. Despite the distance, I truly believe they all became as close to Pop as if they had grown up in Toronto- perhaps even closer. Sometimes, having that one-on-one direct communication that's possible on the telephone provides a level of intimacy you can't always achieve in person.

Because of my experiences raising my own children and helping to care for my grandchildren, I've always wanted to somehow reach other young people to help them grow up. Though I'm sure I wasn't the "perfect" parent all the time, for the most part, I think I've been successful in shaping my children's lives in a positive way. I feel I have helpful advice to offer, but don't know how to get it to these young people. I do hope some of them get a chance to read this book. That might help fulfill this wish of mine to provide some guidance to other youngsters. Maybe it's their parents I should be trying to reach. I don't know. I suppose I just don't like the way most children are being raised today. They seem to have a lack of respect for not only themselves and others, but for everything in society- even their own lives! I'm not certain if this behavior is because of lack of discipline, lack of opportunity, too much free time, too many material goods, or just the fact that the world is a radically different place compared to the one I grew up in. One thing I am certain of, however, is that so many young people don't seem to be happy. They're abusing their bodies, maybe abusing their minds, and I also believe they're abusing their souls. Regardless, a generation without love, hope, and respect doesn't bode well for the future.

One of the things about today's youngsters that saddens me the most is how quickly they turn to drugs and alcohol for happiness. Their family life and upbringing must be missing the kind of nurturing and support I was lucky enough to have if this is the one option they see open for themselves. If only I could convince them they can find happiness and take control of their lives through hard work, education, God, self-examination, or counseling. There are so many other options! It's such a shame for children to waste their talent and intelligence, as well as their futures, because they have no one in their lives to show them a different path. It breaks my heart even more to see these same kids turn to crime and violence to support their drug habits. Then what happens? Not only are they lonely, unhappy people, but they're in jail. If only they knew how different their lives could be, if only someone would teach them how to plan for their future instead of living for the moment.

Kids are not born evil or bad. They become that way because of the way they are raised or how they are treated. I remember Father Flanagan of Boy's Town. His work in the thirties that led to the famous movie in 1938 with Spencer Tracy was all about treating kids right. I don't think you can ever love a child too much, nor can you challenge them enough. I have always believed in dealing with children on a one-to-one basis, virtually as equals. Rocky calls this adult-adult transactional analysis. I call it common sense. So, my good reader, think of your own life. Whenever you were challenged, didn't you feel great when you accomplished your goal? Wasn't it great to run to your mother or father and say, "Hey, look, I did it!" Give your children a chance to do the same thing. Be an example, be a beacon of solidarity, be a beacon of love, but for God's sake, don't molly coddle them. They won't break. Challenge them to excel, to be good, to beat your own records. And also, for God's sake, don't belittle them if they fall or fail. Prop them up. Encourage them to try again, and again, and again. That's what life is all about. More love, more challenge, more support, and more leadership. Then maybe some of our problems will start being solved.

After all, consider the alternatives. These are our children. They are our bridge to the future. They will run this world of ours when we age or die. Let's help them get ready so we can be around to counsel them and feel the sense of accomplishment as they succeed, knowing that we did our job in getting them ready.

I know I wrote earlier in this book about our family philosophy tied to the three dollars a day that we must earn. One dollar to pay our debts in looking after our parents; one dollar to pay our bills today; and one dollar to save for the future by investing in our children.

This world can be such a beautiful place! Sometimes, though, you have to make yourself see beauty. One of the things I learned living through my many tragedies is that you have to keep a positive outlook in order to survive. At times, this can feel like the hardest thing you will ever have to do. But why have a negative attitude? The only person who gets hurt by negative feelings- anger, hatred, jealousy, resentment- is the person with those feelings. I see this as a problem with youngsters too. So many of them are wrong in wanting to jump into a relationship the minute they find a boy or girl who expresses an interest in them. Aside from all the problems that come with pregnancy and sexual diseases, kids are usually not grown up enough to handle the feelings of possessiveness, envy and fear of being alone that such relationships bring with them. At a time when they're desperately looking for love and acceptance, all they find are bad feelings. (I often think starting out your adulthood with such negative thoughts leads to a lifetime of the same). I believe this is where a loving, supportive family is so important. If a child grows up in a caring, unselfish, uncritical atmosphere, the resulting self-esteem and self-confidence that youngster experiences will make all the difference in the world. He or she won't have to search for love and acceptance outside the family.

Again, maybe I should be trying to get my message across to parents. On one hand, children need to know there are other ways to grow up; on the other hand, if parents were themselves better educated about how to raise their kids, maybe young people wouldn't have some of these problems in the first place. I know it's hard for parents today, with divorce so common and the need for both mothers and fathers to work, but I still feel everyone's priorities are somewhat out of whack. Children just don't seem to be as important as they used to. When I was growing up, parents <u>sacrificed</u> for their sons and daughters. Children were rarely, if ever, left alone; in emergencies, other family members would step in. Babysitters, nannies, and daycare centers were almost unheard of! I can't remember Mama or Papa ever leaving me or any of my brothers and sisters alone. Likewise, I never left my children alone. I spent every minute that I wasn't working with them, showing my love in a <u>real</u> way- on a day-to-day basis, giving them all my attention.

I'm really not trying to blame anyone. I honestly just want to help because I love children so much. When I see children who do wrong, I realize it's their circumstances and how they are brought up. When babies are born in the many parts of this planet, they all start out equal, regardless of their race, religion, or whether they're rich or poor. A child is a child. But things like what kind of nutrition they receive, the way they are taught about life and the world by their parents, the type of community they grow up in, and the love they receive from people determines what kind of person they will become as an adult. But deep down, I believe it's truly up to parents to mold the kind of person they want their children to become. Unfortunately, many parents simply lack the knowledge and skills to mold their children properly. It's not their fault; most people only know the child rearing methods (which don't work in our modern society) they've learned from their own parents. Lack of communication, letting anger substitute for discipline, allowing your own needs to take priority over your children's and spoiling them out of guilt or convenience all contribute to a child growing up not feeling cared about. Of course, that's when the problems start, and then it becomes an endless cycle. These children grow up, raise their kids the same way, and nobody's happy and society falls apart. This is why I am so worried about the younger generation- they <u>are</u> the future.

"TIME TO RELAX AND THINK"

Earlier in 1958, as I neared my sixties, my doctors told me that I would have to "take it easy". I'd been active all my life, but did have a history of mild diabetes, had suffered a minor heart attack two years previous and was having increasing difficulty with my balance. For the past few years, I had a problem with my inner ear mechanism- a disease called Meniere's syndrome- that caused severe dizziness at completely unexpected times. I was embarrassed on more than one occasion when I had to grope along the wall like a drunk. Eating salt usually triggered an attack; just eating ham or a salty pretzel was enough to do it. Even stress could cause the disease to act up. It certainly wasn't a very professional image to give, although I must admit to seeing some humor in the situation. Still, not being able to tolerate salt is a pretty tough blow for a chef who prides himself on achieving perfect taste in his dishes. The bottom line was, however, that I would need to retire earlier than I had planned. I worried about how I could survive financially and emotionally if I retired. I knew that at best I would receive only one or two month's salary from my employer, even though I had worked for him for over twenty-three years.

The emotional part was worse. Here I was, fifty-eight, at the height of my ability as a nationally recognized Master Chef, and I was facing the prospect of retiring from my profession. I was still vigorous and full of energy, though. It would be difficult to slow down since work had always been such a vital part of my life. Reluctantly, I decided this was as good a time as any to fully retire. In a way, I suppose I did look forward to having the opportunity to do all the things I never had time for before. Maybe I'd be able to really "enjoy life". Most importantly, it would be a time for me to relax. I never knew the meaning of that word while I was part of the working world. The more I thought about it, the more I believed all this free time would be heavenly. I couldn't have been more wrong. After just a few days of nothing but relaxation, I came down with a wicked case of the boredom blues! If I was going to stay sane, I'd have to keep myself busy.

At least there was plenty for me to do at home. My wife, Bea, had a heart condition and wasn't in the best health. I used to help her with the shopping and household chores. I was always happy to do whatever I could for her.

Bea also never had to set foot in the kitchen, of course, because I did all the cooking with pleasure. I have to admit the best part of retirement was spending so much more time with my wife. I also started thinking about writing several recipe books and travelling, especially a trip back to Italy. Bea was delighted with the idea of going to Italy, so I made the arrangements right away for a voyage in July. Within no time, it was July. Jack and Rocky drove us to New York, where we stayed with my old friend, Mauro Romita, for a few days before leaving. When the day came to depart for Italy, Mauro and his family, Jack, and Rocky came with us, bringing flowers and champagne as bon voyage gifts. We all boarded the ship (the <u>Constitution</u>, an 80,000 ton transatlantic liner- quite a change from the <u>Palermo</u>), and celebrated in the cabin. Everyone on the ship was celebrating too; it was an exciting time! When the ship's whistle blew for the third and final time, Bea and I were left to ourselves.

We stood on deck in the midst of the usual ship departing ceremony with its whistles, sirens, paper tape and shouts of goodbye from the crowds on the dock. As we left port, I could see Jack and Rocky in the crowd and realized I had forgotten to tell them something. I found out later that I could call Toronto directly from my cabin. All I needed to do was just have the ship's switchboard phone the call for me. The following day, I phoned Jack from my cabin. After I gave the switchboard his number in Toronto, it only took about twenty minutes for him to call back. I was talking to him and he thought I was already off the boat. "Where are you?" he said. "I thought I put you on the boat to Italy." We both laughed when I told him I was phoning him from the <u>Constitution</u>. He couldn't believe I was making a phone call from the middle of the Atlantic!

It struck me then as it does now just how much today's technology has created a pleasurable lifestyle for us. It amazes me how in such a short time- my lifetime- there has been this drastic change from the mule-driven carriages, Morse code and simple machinery of my youth to things like space ships, computers, communication satellites and jets. From my perspective, I can still marvel at simple things like making a telephone call from a ship. But the real miracle I see is that people can now enjoy longer, more useful lives. Of all the wonders of modern technology, advances in medicine have been the greatest. In today's world, I probably would not have lost my beloved Peppinella nor our young son or infant daughter.

In 1963, a few years after my phone call, technology brought a very sad moment to all our lives. For the first time in history, the whole world witnessed, through the "miracle" of instant telecommunications, an

American President being murdered. Because of it, businesses closed, classes at schools were cancelled and people openly mourned in the streets for a dead man. When the news of Kennedy's death came to Toronto, I was in Jack's dental office listening to the radio. I jumped right up against the wall in shock and just stood there. I felt as if I didn't know what struck me. It was horrible news, just as if someone in my own family passed away. Plus, to be gunned down without any reason as he was makes such a tragedy that much worse. Tears came to my eyes and I had to use my hanky. "What the heck is next?" I thought. I wondered what the world was coming to when an important statesman like him could be killed so easily.

Rocky happened to be in Toronto that day. Naturally, he was shocked and worried about the news, too. He came over to Jack's office and the three of us listened to the radio as new developments about Kennedy's murder unfolded. I was glad both my sons were with me because I felt a true sense of grief and loss. I could also empathize with the President's father. Such tragedy! Only a father who has lost a son can know what kind of sadness fills a man's heart when a child dies before he does. For the rest of the day- in fact, the next several days- people in Toronto moved about in a daze, stunned. They all felt the same loss as I did. Even though Kennedy wasn't "our" President, the immediacy of his killing and resulting horror that followed was made clear to us through repeated replays of the scene on television. Later, everyone watched the same televisions or listened to the same radios when his funeral was held. The procession was stark, yet moving. When young John-John saluted his father, tears came to my eyes. I almost felt like an intruder, witnessing another family's intimate sorrow like this.

Technology can bring us happy times and sad. It is also capable of bringing us grandeur. Of all the technological advances made in the 60's, the greatest would have to be when the world watched three American astronauts walking on the moon. Television let everyone experience the wonder of these new accomplishments in computer and space science. Just fifty years earlier, journeying to the "New World" meant traveling across an ocean. Now it means traveling into the universe. Because of so many constant technological changes, life itself has changed. Take education for example. When I was growing up, it was unimportant whether you attended school or not. It wasn't even necessary to know how to read! Children learned simple job skills for different trades, along with all the knowledge needed for life, right at home. With today's advanced technology, children must finish high school at the very least just in order to function at a basic level! I got by without a high school or college education because I could learn as I lived. When it came to my profession, my credentials were my ability. Unfortunately, technology has forced us into an age where it has become necessary to possess the "right" paperwork...all too often replacing people's own judgment.

But I do appreciate modern conveniences. When I think of the primitive nature and drabness of life in the early 1900's, I thank God for all the change. Even being able to get any food product from any part of the world while fresh remains a great marvel to me. People should fight a little harder not to sell their souls for money. I believe it's always best to put principle above dollars, and relationships over wealth. I still feel like one of the wealthiest men in the world- wealthy in the knowledge that I'm accepted by my family, friends, and my community because of what I am, not what I own.

Nevertheless, this is a great time to be alive because of scientific achievement but I feel we have lost so much- perhaps even more than we have gained. The pace of life is so fast now and often so artificial. Money seems to be everyone's god, more important than human relationships and family responsibilities. Values and ethics seem to be disappearing in the chase of the almighty dollar as well. Of course, money can buy you technology and technology brings power. It's a difficult thing to fight. In my lifetime, I've been broke more often than "flush", but always felt wealthy. Money can't buy love and I've always had plenty of that from my family. They've given me great comfort and renewed spirit in times of crisis and heightened the grand and glorious times, adding even greater joy to happy occasions. It's so much easier to live a life geared to people rather than money. Don't get me wrong, money is necessary to live, of course, but it's secondary to the closeness and love of family.

Bea and I had a wonderful time throughout that entire trip in 1958. We made some good friends during the crossing, too, with whom we dined every night. During the day, passengers would chat or play cards, shuffleboard, or a variety of games that were available. At night, we gambled (they used dummy horses, of course). Once in a while, the ship held a costume night and everyone made their own costumes. There was also dancing, a bar, and even movies. Bea and I had lots of fun; there was always so much to do. Our meals were also good and the cabin was comfortable. Even better, it was summertime, so the ocean was calm and the weather was clear. The trip took only eight days this time, quite a difference from the twenty day voyage of my previous journey.

As before, the ship landed in Naples. It was brutally hot! I'd forgotten how hot Italy was in the summer! Bea and I took the train to the town of Bari and by the next morning, we were in Modugno. It was marvelous to finally see my sister, Filomena, and two brothers, Nicolo and Raffaele. We had a great family reunion with all my other relatives and memories of my days growing up and previous return visit came flooding back. This time, to my surprise, it was even more difficult to see how narrow the streets really were, how dusty the square was, and how "foreign" the people appeared to me- even my relatives! It dawned on me then that it's best not to go back to a good thing you've left. It's just too sad. If you really love a place, it may be wiser never to go back if you want to keep your memories intact. What made these unexpected feelings even worse was the flood of memories of Peppinella. I had always wanted her to meet my parents and visit Modugno with me, but of course, she never made it.

I made myself put these gloomy thoughts aside. Bea and I were here to enjoy ourselves and I could see no sense in letting myself get depressed over memories. We got into the swing of "being tourists" and spent a great deal of time with my brothers and sister and their children. We stayed in Modugno for three weeks and decided to go to Sicily. Bea still had cousins who lived there, her grandparents having been born in Sicily. We planned on visiting them for a while. Sicily is such a beautiful island. It offers a wide variety of fruits, good farming, good food and buildings full of beauty and history. It was hard for me to equate these friendly people and rustic towns with the stories I'd heard of the crime and power of the Mafia. Perhaps they were organized there, but I didn't see anything out of the ordinary. What I did notice was the heat. August in Sicily is terribly uncomfortable. It's just the distance of the Mediterranean away from North Africa, so I guess I shouldn't have been surprised at the island's climate, but I was.

After Sicily, we travelled to Rome to see Pope Pius XII at his summer home, Castle Gandolfo, some twenty miles north-west of Rome in the Alban Hills. Bea and I were lucky enough to get a pass to visit inside. What a wonderful place! The Castle is truly a castle that was built in the fifteenth century. It rises some four hundred feet above a lake where a small town with stores and restaurants is located. Castle Gandolfo has a set of massive doors located on the main square of town, guarded by the Swiss Guards. Our pass allowed us to be escorted inside the doors and with several other visitors into the inner piazza of the castle. From there, at noon, we all received the blessing of the Pope.

Even at the age of 82, Pope Pius XII was an impressive man who spoke five languages. According to custom, he gave his blessing to us and any gifts or religious objects we had with us. In the native tongues of his audience, he very movingly extended his best wishes to all the members of our families wherever they were. Though he appeared to be physically frail, he spoke for close to an hour, in a clear strong voice. I could see the love for this great man and everything he stood for in everyone's faces. It made me wish I could have known him better. When Bea and I returned to Rome, we heard the Pope had suddenly collapsed. Apparently, we had been at his last audience because a few days later, he died. We both felt a sense of personal loss, as well as the sadness from losing a religious leader. Bea and I made a point to stay for his funeral, a very solemn and moving experience.

I cried that day knowing it had been only a month earlier I had seen him in person. I kept thinking about how kind and attentive he had been to everyone- and there were over a thousand people visiting when Bea and I were there. The Pope held his hands to the sky when he talked and spoke Italian so musically, you couldn't help loving his voice. He hadn't looked or acted like a man ready to die, but God must have had other plans for him. All the Church bells in Italy were ringing and mourning his death on the day of his funeral. Flags were flying at half mast. All over Italy, Catholics had held him in the highest regard and were now grieving for him publicly.

While we were still in Rome, Bea and I took several sightseeing tours. It's utterly amazing to stand at an ancient wall or temple or aqueduct, knowing it was built two thousand years ago, and see for yourself how well it has survived. I have to admit, it was a humbling experience. No matter how impressive modern technology can be, it's awe-inspiring to think that the efforts of those early Romans remain visible today. It just proved how there have always been clever people in the world. You can see unbelievable things in Rome. The selection of fountains, artwork, architecture and sculpture is endless! Though North America is a wonderful country and rich land, everything there has been built or accomplished within the last three hundred years. Almost all the cities in Italy, especially places like Florence and Milan have incredible, complex histories behind them.

Bea and I thoroughly enjoyed everything we did on our trip, but it's a funny thing- all the time I was in Italy, all I could think about was home. I wanted to go home. We finally made plans to leave Italy on the Constitution in October. My nephew came along to see us off at Naples and had supper with us on the ship. They were serving roast beef that night and I asked for an extra cut. Though Italy has excellent food, they don't have roast beef. Did that ever taste good! Bea though I was crazy. On the day we were to arrive in New York, I got up at 3:30 and went on deck. I wanted to see the Statue of Liberty as we sailed into New York harbor. I cried as I saw the statue and kissed the deck as the ship passed by it. I was home and glad to be there.

"FACING YOUR OWN MORTALITY"

For practically all of my life, I've been healthy. I've always tried to be good to myself and my body. Though I did make some mistakes in the past, fortunately I learned from them. When I was twenty-one, I went to see a doctor for the first time in my life because I hadn't been felling well for several months. As it happened, my illness was self-inflicted. I weighed over three hundred pounds and had dumped so much sugar in my system that I caused my own diabetes. The doctor gave me a choice between taking insulin for the rest of my life or losing a lot of weight and staying away from sweets. I chose the latter. Today, my weight is under control. I never eat sweets and have never needed one dose of insulin. I also used to be a fairly heavy smoker. My doctor never advised me to quit (it wasn't always known how hazardous cigarettes were to your health) and I never really thought about the dangers of smoking until they literally hit me in the face. I was sitting in traffic one day with Jack, smoking a cigarette and listening to a program on the radio about air pollution. Our car was behind a truck and the combination of diesel and gasoline fumes, plus my cigarette smoke, made the air so thick we could hardly breathe without gagging! At that moment, it dawned on me how stupid I had been to smoke. No more cigarettes for me! I threw out the rest of that pack and never smoked again.

Despite smoking and having diabetes, I never missed a day of work due to illness until the day I had my first heart attack at fifty-six. After leaving work one day, I went to Jack's dental office for a visit. Walking towards his front door, I suddenly felt out of breath and sat on the steps for a few moments before going in. The pain started as I sat there. It felt like a ton of bricks was resting in the center of my chest. Jack saw me, took one look and immediately called the hospital telling them to expect an emergency. He virtually picked me up and carried me to his car. Within minutes, I was in the emergency room at St. Michael's where I was diagnosed with a heart attack.

It was a little scary lying there. I was only fifty-six years old and still had so much yet to do. Without warning, I was being told I was lucky to be alive. Throughout my heart attack I hadn't really been afraid, nor was I afraid of being in the hospital. I suppose I had seen death so many times close up that it no longer held any fear for me. But I was sad and apprehensive thinking that I might not live to see my grandchildren.

Jack had just adopted a beautiful little girl, and Rocky had recently completed his doctorate studies and would be ready to start a family soon, too. I wanted desperately to survive so I could hold, play with and love my new grandchild and future grandchildren. Death had already intruded into my life so many times already, like a thief stealing my loved ones away from me. Now, it was trying to rob me of the future I craved.

I know everyone is mortal. Death is our destiny. None of us can avoid it and we can only delay it by being wise and careful. But knowing this didn't make me feel any better. The doctors told me I would have to slow down. I argued with both them and myself- <u>this</u> wasn't the time! I didn't yet have the financial means to survive without working, and I felt too young and energetic to quit. But my doctors were adamant; so were my sons. Apparently, I had suffered significant heart damage and my history of diabetes complicated matters. So I listened to what they all said and wondered if I was really "all-washed up" at fifty-six.

Because of Bea's heart problem, I asked Jack not to tell her about the seriousness of my condition. Like all concerned wives, however, she eventually worried the whole story out of us. (At least for the first few days anyway, Bea and I talked by phone; I didn't want her rushing to the hospital and having an attack herself). Jack did call Rocky that day and he arrived from Montreal later in the evening. That night, the three of us sat and talked quietly in my hospital room. A number of doctor friends dropped in. They all said the same thing: "Take it easy". The next morning I felt much better. The pain was gone and I felt myself again. The nurses told me I was allowed out of bed, so I walked gingerly down the corridors of my floor. As I looked around at the sick and dying, I resolved to get out of that hospital as soon as possible, whether I was better or not! If I was going to die, I wanted to die in my own bed. Bea agreed with me. In less than a week, I was released and went home.

A month later, I felt as strong as ever, but my diabetes and inner ear disease started making me terribly dizzy. I wobbled whenever I walked. Again, I was advised by doctors to retire and give up my job as a Master Chef. At this point, I had been working steadily for forty-two years and was not about to just up and quit. Jack and Rocky insisted they would provide any financial support I needed but I absolutely did not want to be a burden on them. Instead, I decided to "semi-retire" and seek easier employment, perhaps as a consultant. I could retain my editorship of the monthly column for the *Canadian Hotel and Restaurant Review* and continue as a culinary judge. This way, I could stay active in my profession without the physical drain of running a restaurant.

Unfortunately, my plan didn't work. First of all, I had no pension. I was continually worried about finances. Secondly, I was bored out of my mind. I had just enough cash to pay my bills for two years, and Jack was insisting he needed me in his practice as his general manager and aide. Rocky also wanted me to take this job if for no other reason than to look after Jack and make sure he didn't work too hard. So there I was, a retired Master Chef working in a dental practice! Needless to say, it was a big change for me. It's hard to get used to being a worker again when you've been in command for most of your life. Jack couldn't have been a nicer or more patient employer, but it was his show. I missed the excitement and responsibility of being the center of things, but I had no choice. I made the best of it.

In 1961, Rocky finally married a wonderful young lady from Philadelphia. The minute I met her I knew she was the girl for him. He was thirty-two and she was twenty-two, but they were a perfect match. I happily contemplated the possibility of more grandchildren as their wedding approached. I started feeling ill again. I noticed my hands had dark blotches on them. Soon, my forearms were covered with warts and black moles. My doctor told me I had a form of "melanoma", or skin cancer. The kind I had was called Kaposes Sarcoma. I remembered that back in the fifties, I had a black mole close to my right eye that suddenly grew to three times its size. During a doctor's visit, he put some ether on it to anesthetize it prior to a biopsy. While he was gone, I felt around the mole with my finger and gradually worked at it until it fell off. When the doctor returned, he was horrified but then elated because he said it looked like the entire growth had come out. Hopefully, he said, none of its cells had been left to re-grow. I thought that possibly my current problem might have been a result of that episode. I saw many specialists and they all told me the same thing. It was a slow-acting cancer that is common in southern Mediterranean areas where people are exposed to too much sun, especially as children. They also told me that in someone my age, it could be controlled with radiation treatments. Since there was nothing I could really do about the melanoma, I simply chose not to worry about it. What good would worrying do? Every month or so, especially as the warts got bigger, I had them surgically removed. I also went ahead with the radiation treatments, which I didn't care for because the

X-rays seemed to affect my whole body. At first, they visibly burned the skin on my arms and legs. Eventually, though, the doctors got it under control.

Although I did my best to try "taking it easy", this was just too foreign to my nature. Being active and involved had always been a large part of my life. One incident in particular happened where I just couldn't help myself and it led to a second heart attack. I even made the headlines of the Toronto Star! It was twelve years after my first heart attack and I had been chosen for jury duty. I told the judge my health history, but also told him I felt fine. The case was to be a major murder trial. As a juror, I soon became all too familiar with the gory circumstances of the murder. A young man in his late twenties was married to a beautiful young girl of twenty-one. He was accused of strangling her in a bathtub. His alleged motive was to collect on her life insurance policy. This man's defense was that his wife had taken a radio with her into her bath and been accidentally electrocuted when it fell into the water.

For the two weeks the trial lasted, I worried over how I had this man's life in my hands. I listened intently to 80 witnesses for the prosecution. She had died from strangulation, not electrocution; he had beaten her before witnesses on more than one occasion; he sought a prostitute during his wife's wake; and the insurance policy had been issued only a few weeks before the victim's death. I listened, considered, debated and searched for the truth. I felt a great responsibility to be absolutely sure of my decision. At last, the defendant himself took the stand. He sneered at everyone in the courtroom. I remember the prosecuting attorney asking him, "How do you explain the 80 witnesses who have testified against you?" He answered in a cocky shout, "They all lied!" At that moment, I became <u>furious</u> at this self-centered, smart-mouthed, cunning rogue. His conviction was instantly clear in my mind. This scoundrel had murdered a young innocent girl for money! That's all I remember. Apparently, I rose out of my seat in anger and passed out right there in the courtroom. Within moments, I was back at St. Michael's with another heart attack.

This time, I felt like a pro. Being in the hospital was the least of my concerns. To think I had worried for days about being fair to this despicable person. They way he shouted, "They all lied!" kept playing over and over in my mind. The doctors, however, were seriously worried about me- so worried that they arranged for me to be given the "Last Rites" of the Catholic faith. At that point, I suppose I did start to wonder if I would survive. I was given the last rites of the church. Having the "Last Rites" administered does tend to wake you up to the fact of your own mortality. Suddenly, I felt a sense of urgency to make sure the arrangements for my death would be in order if I did die. I discussed my feeling about the situation with Bea and the boys. I wanted to be buried in the family plot I had purchased when Peppinella had died. She was there along with our two dead children. There was room for Bea and even Jack and Rocky.

As painful as all this was, I felt it necessary to plan ahead. Both of my sons explained they wanted to be buried in their own family plots when the time came, and Bea told me that she, too, had a family plot and suggested I consider being buried there with her. It's strange how little personal details like that can suddenly become a source of bother and anxiety. I was saddened, but knew I wanted to be buried with Peppinella and our son and daughter. I made my decision and I let Bea and the boys know. Jack, as my executor, promised to carry out my wishes.

I was still upset from the stress of the trial and these discussions hadn't exactly helped me to relax. My doctors told me point blank that I was tense and had to calm down or risk suffering another attack. My sons thought of a perfect way to help me get started. They showed me the newspaper with the headline and story about my passing out in the courtroom. The idea of this made me laugh and I began to feel the tension leave my body. To think I had to have a heart attack to make headlines. What a way to be noticed, and noticed I was! People I hadn't seen or heard from in years flocked to the hospital, phoned, or sent gifts. In the meantime, the doctors were constantly lecturing me about slowing down. Under no circumstances was I to overexert myself or was I to lift anything heavy. From now on I would have to avoid stress, fatigue and excitement. I also had to eliminate all fat from my diet. But the worst thing was that for the second time I was faced with retirement- and this time, full retirement.

Rocky and Jack, of course, were just as urgent in their pleas for me to retire. They suggested I write a major book on recipes for entertaining- formal dinners and parties held at home. They also urged me to dictate thoughts and reminiscences of my life. (Rocky even started right there in the hospital with a tape recorder asking me questions about Modugno. Just thinking about the happy times of my youth seemed to speed my recovery). The idea of creating entertainment recipes struck me right away as a good one, and did give me something to look forward to. I started working on the book as soon as I got home from the hospital. Checking the recipes to make sure their ingredients worked was a tedious thing to do but they had to be right. Bea and I worked together on them. She was a tremendous help to me. We had numerous dinners for friends so they could sample all the new dishes I created. I also gave away countless numbers of pies and cakes as I experimented with different ideas and special ways of decorating them. As always, I made sure every recipe was aromatic, tasty, and looked good.

Naturally, I found out I really enjoyed working on the recipe book. I have always loved to cook because it's such a creative process. It truly requires the skills of the artist: selection, creativity, imaginative presentation and the idea that you can make something perfect. There is also the satisfaction that comes from seeing any masterpiece prepared and presented for sharing. However, where the painter, writer, musician or poet may work in solitude for long periods of time before their work can be either appreciated or rejected by an audience, cooking is much more immediate and certainly less solitary. The Master Chef can create, compare, adjust and improve all within a very short period of time. I loved being a chef. I loved the challenge, the artistry, the human reaction- the reaction even more so because it was always one-on-one. Even with something as simple as lettuce for a salad, it has to sound crisp, be crisp, look crisp, smell crisp and taste crisp. The perfect dish speaks for itself immediately. If it doesn't, the diner always knows.

Working on these recipes became a great challenge and eventually the new focus of my life. Even nicer, Bea and I became extremely close. Working with her like this gave our relationship an added dimension it didn't have before. We continued to work together on my first cookbook until she died in September of 1975. Bea had always had a heart condition, but was careful and took very good care of herself. Her sudden death came as a severe shock to me. I was honestly surprised. It just never occurred to me she might die before me. Bea had always come across as competent and having everything under control. After dinner one night, Bea went outside to play with our dog. Later, as she walking back up the steps into the house, she simply collapsed having dropped dead of a massive heart attack. Her death struck a nerve in me. Life became difficult to cope with. I was retired, home alone all the time, and dearly missed my wife. At a time when I longed for intimate companionship the most, I was left with none. After Bea died, I've continued to live in our house, keeping the place neat, and fixing my own meals. Every now and then, I still feel the pangs of loneliness from missing Bea, but quickly realize that I'm never truly alone. Jack and his family live across the street and Rocky phones and visits me often. When they're not around, I find comfort in knowing God is always with me.

I suffered a third heart attack when I was seventy-two and Bea was still alive. I was on the way to the doctor's office for my monthly checkup. I always took the subway downtown and then dutifully walked to the hospital. This particular time, it was February and bitterly cold, so I snuck into a nearby department store to walk part of the way indoors. Suddenly, a woman in front of me fainted. No one bothered to go help her. I hollered for help, but sill no one came. By that point, I just didn't see where I had any choice. I knelt down to check on her, raised her legs, talked to her until she came to, and finally helped her sit up. Then I felt faint! At last, an emergency team arrived. Of course, I asked them to take care of the woman first, but they were more worried about me. So was she. Apparently, I was turning blue. The ambulance personnel administered oxygen and gave me an injection through a vein. My heart seemed all right. I wasn't having any chest pain but there was something else terribly wrong. Maybe I had strained myself lifting the woman. I was weak and felt very faint. Again, I was rushed to St. Michael's Hospital. I guess I must have been in a delicate state because my family wasn't even allowed to talk to me.

EDITOR'S NOTE: That night, when I arrived at his beside from New York, I asked Pop, "Why?" His answer was typically Pop: "The lady fell down. Nobody was helping her. I had to!" I told him it was a stupid thing to do, but wonderful. I was proud of him, but concerned over what he might do next to help others at his own expense.

It was a long night. He wasn't expected to live. By God, he did though, and for more than nine years.

It was a bad night for me. Everyone thought I was going to die and wouldn't even make it through until morning. If any of my family came to visit, they could only stay for two minutes each. I have to admit, this time I was actually scared myself. I was given the last rites (again) and started to have a serious dialogue in my mind. About four o'clock in the morning, I thought, "Domenic, you're finished." Nevertheless, I was prepared. This was life; death is a natural part of it. I wasn't bitter about anything or angry at anyone. I never have been. I thought about how I was content and satisfied because of the full, happy life I led. On the other hand, I was sad; again, because I felt I still had lots of important things to do- be with my grandchildren, be with my friends, take care of Bea and finish my cookbook. It wasn't time yet. It's strange how certain thoughts come to you when you think you're going to die. Finally, it hit me: "You know what you've got to do", I said to myself. "You've got to fight like the other times. Fight! You'll survive!" A little while later, I thought, "Aw, Domenic, go to sleep. You're not going to die. You're going to be fine, like always." On and on this dialogue went until I seemed almost to just take a deep breath and suddenly relax. I decided that what is meant to be will be and to let God take care of it. By daybreak, my crisis was over. I had survived my third heart attack. I stayed in the hospital for three weeks. Bea and Jack came to visit every day. Rocky stayed for a week and then had to return to New York, keeping in touch by phone.

When I did make it home, I was limited to staying in bed for several more weeks. I wasn't out of the house all winter long. It also seemed to be an unusually cold winter that year. The frigid air always managed to burn its way right through to my bones. I couldn't seem to keep warm no matter what I did. In the spring, I started moving around the house carefully, sometimes playing outside with the dog. I did little chores inside and started going for short walks with Bea. When I turned seventy-three in July, it seemed to be a turning point for me. I started to improve rapidly, recovering my zest for living. A little at a time I started working on my recipe book again; the more I worked, the better I felt. Once more, I had a purpose to my life and put my troubles behind me. I found out it's always better to do something, no matter what, and be involved than to mope around waiting to die.

For the next two years, I couldn't do as much as I wanted but put a lot of effort into the cookbook. Unfortunately, I discovered there was more attention to the little details of writing a book required than I could handle in my restricted condition. The last time I had published a new book, it was for the company who owned *Canadian Hotel and Restaurant Review* and they handled the business details. Though I knew I had created many excellent recipes and there were good things in the book for its readers, I didn't feel quite capable of delivering it to the public because I wasn't a professional writer. Still, despite my doubts and uncertainties, I persisted. I finally finished the book, although in handwritten form. With the recipes all tested, I started searching for a publisher.

Now that I was spending more time at home and the book was done as well, I used my extra time for reading as much as I could. One night, I noticed an unusual dimness while reading the newspaper. As each day passed, it became harder and harder to read. Images grew fuzzy. I went to my family doctor first about this problem, and he referred me to an eye specialist, a Dr. Eugene Kelly. Dr. Kelly was almost my age and was a thorough, kind man. "Dominic," he said, "you have a cataract in each eye. I don't want to operate yet because your vision's not bad enough. In the meantime, you've got two or three years of living with progressive sight impairment before I can justify performing the surgery."

EDITOR'S NOTE: Cataract surgery was considered much more complicated in the 1970's. Unlike today, where it can usually be performed on an outpatient basis, this surgery used to be categorized as a major procedure, not to be taken lightly. Pop not only waited two years for his first operation, but spent ten days in the hospital afterwards. It was not an easy event.

His diabetes, while under control, was a contributing factor to the formation of his cataracts and would also affect how quickly he healed. That, together with his cardiovascular history and problems with melanoma, did not make him an ideal patient. The awful part of all this was that Pop feared things like blindness and helplessness whereas he never really feared death.

Fortunately for everyone, Gene Kelly was a thoughtful and extremely talented eye surgeon. As anyone could see by the great smile that lit his face when he was successful with his patients, Dr. Kelly was a genuinely caring human being. I always felt grateful for how he helped Pop.

So, for the next two years I coped with progressive blindness. It eventually got so bad that I couldn't even see across the room or even barely make out my hand when I held it in front of my face. Reading was really tough, nearly impossible. I bought the biggest, strongest magnifying glass I could find and increased the power of the light bulbs all over the house. With the bright light and my "glass", I somehow managed to read, but it was slow going. Getting around to my daily chores was a different story. I refused to carry a cane, so I just walked slower and groped my way along, even in my own home. I rarely went anywhere alone, and certainly never downtown. Jack and his wife were a very great help, always taking me anywhere I had to go, especially for medical treatments. Rocky started visiting more often to keep me company during the long boring times when I just sat at home. One good thing that came of all this was my rediscovering the joy of good music. I picked up whistling again and began challenging the canary to duets. As usual, Bea thought I was crazy. I whistled all kinds of tunes- classical, popular, operatic- but not rock. I even whistled and sang "O Solo Mio" in the Caruso style- a la Martino!

Those two years passed very slowly. It took all my energy and willpower to remain optimistic and motivated throughout what I think of as the longest time in my life. While everyone wanted to help me, I continually felt like a burden, which I hated. To some extent, I got over this because I finally realized that it gave people, my family in particular, a chance to do something for me, return my love and make themselves feel good. That change in outlook helped me a great deal. I suspect that too often people feel ashamed to accept the love that others want to show them, and worse, end up hurting these same persons by rejecting their attention. I found out that by accepting love, both you and the giver feel terrific! Anyway, Dr. Kelly operated on my right eye in the spring of 1975. When the bandages came off, I could see! What an incredible thrill! I almost cried when I took Dr. Kelly's hands in mine, and asked God to bless this good man and his skill. At once, I felt life was worth living again.

I was anxious to have the same surgery done on my left eye as soon as possible. Regrettably, before he could operate, Dr. Kelly became ill and died. A second blow hit me when Bea died. Tragedy seemed to be stalking me again. It wasn't until the following year that my other eye was operated on. But, as often happens with cataract surgery, this procedure wasn't as successful. Though I was out of the hospital in two days, within a week, I had a "vitreous hemorrhage" (a blood clot in the fluid inside the eye). As a result of the hemorrhage, I was intermittently blind off and on in my left eye and have suffered with this ever since.

I must admit, the past few years have been lonely ones for me, especially without Bea. While I've always enjoyed the independence of living in my own home and feel secure being in familiar, comfortable surroundings, I also feel terribly alone. I do find comfort and a certain satisfaction in keeping busy and dictating these reminiscences. Mostly, I spend a lot of time on the telephone (usually every day) talking to my sons, their families and my sister, Mary. I also phone my friends regularly. I talk to my sister Mary every day, often two or three times. The telephone has become my link to my loved ones and friends all over Canada and the United States. It's been my way to "keep in touch" with life. I think my pride keeps me going too…that and a little bit of fear! None of us wants to be alone and none of us wants to be left in a parking lot waiting to die. (That's what I think of nursing homes). No matter how comfortable, new, clean or expensive they are, being in a nursing home can't compare to living in your own familiar surroundings. Nothing really belongs to you and no one can take care of you as well as you can for yourself. You're constantly at the mercy of others. Sure, living on my own is more difficult at my age, but I've considered the options and none of them appeal to me.

Even moving to a retirement community or living with one of my sons is totally out of the question. I could never allow myself to become a burden on anyone! I've spent my whole life taking care of myself and don't intend to change now. I not only need to be free, but I'm afraid not to be.

My other constant worry is money. No matter how much my children reassure me they'll always be there to take care of me, I still worry about the bills and what would happen if Rocky or Jack became unable to help. Despite my worries, I recognize that I also have many wonderful things in my life to sustain me. My grandchildren come to mind immediately. My greatest joy is to see them, speak to them, and gauge the effect I have on their lives. I think we all can see ourselves reborn in our children, but especially so in our grandchildren. In a way, it's like we're viewing our own immortality. I am also sustained by my faith in God, my memories and my optimism. I often think of the young children I tried to help at the Hospital for Sick Children and Home for the Incurable. I've been able to live a full life, while many of them never got started.

Naturally, my religious beliefs sustained me as well. Though I never wore my faith on my sleeve, I've always believed in a loving God, much like Papa, who guides me, helps me and points me in the right direction. My God is a very personal God whom I can talk to "man to man", so to speak. I've always believed priests, ministers, rabbis and all good and holy people are servants of God, just as you an I are but that they're not always necessary in order for a person to be close to God. Neither have I ever been "hung up" or snobbish about different religions or denominations. Faith itself is the important thing. Believing in God has helped me face difficulty so often in my lifetime that I wish everyone had the benefit of a holy presence in their lives. My religion is a quiet religion that has brought me peace and understanding in life and comfort as I begin to face death.

When it comes to simply coping from day to day, I just make sure I keep busy- and keeping busy is easy. Between talking on the phone, watching television, reading, dictating and cooking, I certainly do stay active. I love to bake pies or pastries and then call my neighbors over for coffee and sweets. I still enjoy watching people relish my cooking. It also gives me joy to send pies and cakes to anyone who is sick. I try to entertain as much as I can, even if it's just small dinners for friends or family.

> EDITOR'S NOTE: Pop was always great to me, but whenever I visited him in Toronto, he prepared a sumptuous banquet fit for a king. Dinner lasted for hours as we thoroughly enjoyed the meal, the company, and the jokes. Pop had a tremendous sense of humor and of course, was so wonderful to be with because of his upbeat nature. He was a walking repository of funny stories, sagacious advice, interesting opinions and sound counsel. I often discussed business problems with him. Even though he didn't understand the technical aspects, he always seemed to be able to get to the heart of the matter. His advice certainly influenced the outcome of many tough projects I was working on.

In my experience, the worst thing about growing old is the constant reminder of your own mortality as more and more friends and relatives pass away. This holds especially true for me when members of the family died- my brothers, sisters, cousins, aunts and uncles. An entire era passed when Peppinella's mother, Annunziata, died. She was ninety-six and had lived the last two years of her life with a pacemaker implanted in her heart. To the end, she was a powerful woman, yet despite our differences in the past, I still miss her. Throughout my life, family was the key. I loved and was loved by my family at all times. Their love and caring supported me in illness and tragedy, just as I tried to support other family members in theirs. My own and my wives' families were a solid, secure unit. We all helped each other and worked together for common goals. That isn't to say we didn't fight or never got angry at one another, but we always overcame our problems because we knew family had to come first. Your family should be something you can always count on, no matter what.

In dictating these memories of my life, I've often found it easier to describe the pranks, adventures, successes and joys. The tragedies were more difficult. It was hard to remember and relive the inner turmoil I felt witnessing the deaths of a son, a daughter, and two wives. Words can never truly express such deep sorrow. Nor can I ever truly erase the memory of these events, even after all these years. But I hope my memories have helped to create a bond between me and you, the reader- the bond of one human to another. Maybe my experiences can be a source of inspiration and if you like, a guide for living or an adventure yarn, if you prefer. Then again, my tale may simply be a lesson in family love.

There is so much more that I would like to write about, but I'm afraid this is too long already. I have so many happy memories of all my brothers, their weddings, their children, and yes, their deaths. Of my sisters, Angeline and Filomena, and of course my sister/daughter Maria. So many memories, so many good times, so many occasions when we all felt the need of each other, and the support. For me throughout my life, the family was first. Thank God for the legacy I inherited from my wonderful parents.

I'll be eighty in July. That's a long time to spend on this good earth. I've come from being a shoe shine boy to a Master Chef. People often ask me what my secret is for how I've been able to live so long. Believe it or not, I find this an easy question to answer. First of all, I feel I've been lucky. For the most part,

God has chosen to be good to me. Though I've had my share of heartaches, the suffering has always been bearable and the good times have far outweighed the bad. More importantly, I look upon life as a continual learning experience. Everyone makes mistakes, but these can be made useful if people learn from them. In the same way, we are all given crosses to bear and can learn how to live with them, as well as from them. We must. If we don't, life will never be very pleasant. I've had to make many changes and unpleasant adjustments in my lifetime. It wasn't easy, but nothing worthwhile ever is.

Do I have any special advice for those who want to live to a ripe old age? Know yourself. Respect yourself. Have confidence in yourself. It's as simple as that. If you have these things, serenity will follow. Everything falls into place if you focus on the good things in life, surround yourself with hope and sustain your spirit with love- love of family, love of God and love of country. There is a basic joy to life that you must never let tragedy or misfortune obscure. Serenity allows you to accept what you can't change, and then gives you strength to change what you can. The wisdom that comes with age usually lets you know which is which. So, take care of your health, don't worry about those things you can't control and most importantly, learn how to adapt to whatever life tosses your way.

That's my secret. It's nothing revolutionary, and I didn't find it hidden among the world's treasures. Life is the most priceless treasure I own and I intend to be around for a long, long time!

EDITOR'S NOTE: Pop died two and a half years later. He did no further dictating after his eightieth birthday. He and I reviewed transcripts and made a few family videotapes, most of them shot at our summer home by my son, Paul. Pop really believed he would live until his hundredth birthday. Tragically, his melanoma finally caught up with him. In November of 1982, he developed a very serious infection in his right leg. The last X-ray treatment he received had burned him terribly. The incisions to remove his warts had further left his leg a bloody mess. Finally, Jack and I took him to Toronto's Princess Margaret Hospital, which specialized in cancer care. The hospital's well-known specialists provided him treatment but no courtesy. They assumed that since Pop was eighty-two, he had lived a full life and wasn't a priority. For them, he was a nursing problem rather than a patient. My brother and I were justifiably aggravated by their attitude, but our hands were tied; we did the best we could. At one point, we thought we had conquered both Pop's illness and the arrogance of the health care system, having demanded blood tests that proved he had an electrolyte deficiency that was affecting him. An infusion of saline solution solved the problem and, at least for a few days, he was better. By then, Pop's leg was healing. Everyone hoped and prayed he would be home for Christmas of 1982. It was not to be. On Saturday, December 11th, at about 3:30 in the afternoon while I was with him, he had a massive pleural embolism and died in a second. One quiet sigh and Pop's long life was over.

Pop summed up his own life before he died. He was surrounded and sustained by the love of his family and the love of God. I hope his life will shine as a beacon to others showing what good can come from a single lifetime- one lived quietly, without fanfare, without excessive wealth. Pop was a hero of life's little things done well. He fiercely loved and was loved fiercely in return. I hope he knows how much he's missed!

EPILOGUE

AUNT MARY'S TRIP TO AMERICA

EDITOR'S NOTE: My Aunt Mary had memories of her own, regarding her trip to America:

"I was hesitant and upset about leaving my parents in Italy. I knew they planned on coming to Canada later but begged them to let me delay my departure until I could go with them. They insisted, however, that I leave early to help prepare the way. It was with a real sense of foreboding that I said goodbye to them, because while I knew they were scheduled to leave in a few months, there was a dull ache of uncertainty in my heart. The rumors of war were starting to swirl around but people were convinced that somehow or other peace would prevail. Everyone was also optimistic because of the Munich Accord in 1938 when Neville Chamberlain flew to Munich and met with Hitler arriving at an agreement with him. During that time, Mussolini had stood by Britain helping to convince Germany to back down. As much as we disliked Mussolini (our family was strongly anti-fascist), we hoped that his continued support of Britain would keep Hitler backing down. Of course, we were all shocked when not only did Mussolini withdraw his support from Britain, but Neville Chamberlain presented an ultimatum to Germany and backed it up with a declaration of war. I was heartbroken because I knew war would prevent Mama and Papa from leaving Modugno.

For me, life was dramatically different in Canada. I had gone from being a coddled youngest child to taking on the adult responsibility of caring for two young boys.

Jack was shy with a wonderful smile. He could never do enough for me. He helped me hang clothes, wash floors and do whatever chores needed doing around the house all through that first summer. Rocky was a typical ten year old but with the strangest eating habits. He would eat nothing but hot dogs and tomato soup if he could get away with it. I felt sorry for him not having a mother but I knew that somehow I had to get him to eat vegetables. He was as thin as a rail and insistently kept asking for hot dogs and more hot dogs. I just as equally insisted he eat the vegetables I put on his plate. Throughout the summer, we gradually came to an agreement that he'd eat vegetables half the time if I made hot dogs and tomato soup half the time.

On the other hand, my brother Domenic was very nervous about having me in the house. He had only raised boys and had no experience with teenage girls. Fortunately for him, though, I didn't have much of an opportunity to date for the first few years because most of the young men were joining the service to fight in World War II. Everywhere I went in 1939, I saw men and women in uniform. Toronto became the air training center for the entire Allied Forces, so I often saw airmen from all over the world- New Zealand,

Australia, Poland, Czechoslovakia, Norway, Holland, and all the others.

It wasn't until the early 1940's that I finally met Andy Mencarelli, my husband-to-be. I can still remember our first date. Domenic had insisted that I be home by 11:00 P.M. When I complained loud and long, he finally relented and agreed to 11:30. Andy and I had gone to a movie and it ran a little late so we didn't pull up to the house until 11:40. As I was talking to Andy and he was asking me when we could go out again, I saw Domenic out of the corner of my eye walking onto the porch carrying a milk bottle. He shook the bottle and I could hear the tinkle of money inside it. I wondered why Domenic had put money in the milk bottle until I realized it was his way of giving me a signal that I was late. I immediately burst out laughing and told Andy what was going on. Just as he started laughing too, Domenic came out again with another milk bottle with coins in it and shook it just as vigorously and put it down beside the other one. He kept adjusting the two bottles, clinking them together until he finally just put them down and went inside. Eventually, I went in and asked Domenic why he needed two quarts of milk for the next day. He just replied, "Oh." He went outside, took the money out of the bottles, and brought one in. He never gave me the "signal" again.

APPENDIX A

POP'S OBITUARY

DOMENICO MARTINO WAS MASTER CHEF

Domenico Martino, 82, was an award-winning master chef known professionally for his flair in the kitchen, and privately for his love of children.

He died at Princess Margaret Hospital Saturday after a short illness.

Martino became one of the few Canadians to be recognized worldwide as a master chef when he was elected to the International Epicurean Circle of London in 1957.

But for most of his life, he worked to promote the restaurant industry in Canada. He was food editor of the *Canadian Restaurant and Hotel Review* for 10 years until 1958, as well as a monthly columnist for the publication. He was featured twice as their cover story.

2 Cook Books

He wrote two cook books, *Recipes for Chefs*, published by Maclean-Hunter in 1952, and *More Recipes for Chefs*, published four years later.

From 1953 to 1963 he served as a senior judge at the annual Canadian Culinary Food Show and Exhibition. He was also a founding director and officer of the Canadian Food Services Executive Association.

In 1947, he was founding chef of the Silver Rail Restaurant in Toronto and remained there until he retired in 1956.

Although Martino was devoted to his profession, he gave much of his free time to children. For years, he ran movies for children every Friday night at the Hospital for Sick Children. He also organized Halloween and Valentine's Day dinners for children suffering from incurable diseases.

Staff of 300

"He was a tremendous man for children and a strong supporter of all youth activities," said his son, Dr. Rocco Martino. "That's what he really concentrated on."

Born in Modugno, Italy, Martino came to Canada in 1913 with his father. After finishing school, he traveled across the country cooking in lumber camps and for the railroad.

After he married in 1925, Martino began working in hotels. By 1929, he had taken over as chief chef at Brant's Inn and had a staff of 300.

He was also a chef at the Royal York Hotel and the King Edward Hotel.

Recently, he had been working on an autobiography based on his early years in Canada.

He leaves sons Dr. Jiacoma Martino and Dr. Rocco Martino, five grandchildren and a great-granddaughter.

A funeral will be held tomorrow at 10:30 am at St. Margaret's Queen of Scotland Church on Avenue Road.

TORONTO STAR, TUESDAY, DECEMBER 14, 1982

Domenico Martino was master chef

Domenico Martino, 82, was an award-winning master chef known professionally for his flair in the kitchen, and privately for his love of children.

He died at Princess Margaret Hospital Saturday after a short illness.

Martino became one of the few Canadians to be recognized worldwide as a master chef when he was elected to the International Epicurian Circle of London in 1957.

But for most of his life, he worked to promote the restaurant industry in Canada.

He was food editor of the Canadian Restaurant and Hotel Review for 10 years until 1958, as well as a monthly columnist for the publication. He was featured twice as their cover story.

2 cook books

He wrote two cook books, Recipes for Chefs, published by Maclean-Hunter in 1952, and More Recipes for Chefs, published four years later.

From 1953 to 1963 he served as a senior judge at the annual Canadian Culinary Food Show and Exhibition. He was also a founding director and officer of the Canadian Food Services Executive Association.

In 1947, he was founding chef of the Silver Rail Restaurant in Toronto and remained there until he retired in 1956.

Although Martino was devoted

Obituaries

Domenico Martino: Devoted free time to children.

to his profession, he gave much of his free time to children. For years, he ran movies for children every Friday night at the Hospital for Sick Children. He also organized Hallowe'en and Valentine's Day dinners for children suffering from incurable diseases.

Staff of 300

"He was a tremendous man for children and a strong supporter of all youth activities," said his son, Dr. Rocco Martino. "That's what he really concentrated on."

Born in Modugno, Italy, Martino came to Canada in 1913 with his father. After finishing school, he travelled across the country cooking in lumber camps and for the railroad.

After he married in 1925, Martino began working in hotels. By 1929, he had taken over as chief chef at Brant's Inn and had a staff of 300.

He was also a chef at the Royal York Hotel and the King Edward Hotel.

Recently, he had been working on an autobiography based on his early years in Canada.

He leaves sons Dr. Jiacoma Martino and Dr. Rocco Martino, five grandchildren and a great-grand-daughter.

A funeral will be held tomorrow at 10.30 a.m. at St. Margaret's Queen of Scotland Church on Ave-

211

TORONTO STAR, TUESDAY, DECEMBER 14, 1982

MARTINO, Domenico— At Princess Margaret Hospital Toronto on Saturday, December 11, 1982. Domenico Martino in his 83rd year. Beloved husband of the late Josephine Di Giulio and the late Pietrina Barone. Loving father of Dr. Jiacomo Martino and his wife Betty and Dr. Rocco Martino and his wife Barbara. Beloved grandfather of Jo-Anne (Mrs. J. D.Gallagher), Midshipman Peter, Joseph, Paul and John Martino. Beloved Nonno of great-granddaughter Beth Gallagher. Brother of Michele, Raffaele, Maria (Mrs. M. Mencarelli) and the late Angela Bungaro, Filomena Balenzano, Francesco and Nicolo Martino. Mr. Martino will be resting at the Trull Funeral Home, 2704 Yonge St. at Alexandra Blvd. after 2 p.m. Monday. A Funeral Mass at St. Margaret's Queen of Scotland Church, (Avenue Rd. S. of Wilson) Wednesday 10:30 a.m. Interment Mt. Hope Cemetery. In lieu of flowers memorial donations to the Hospital for Sick Children, 555 University Ave. would be appreciated.

APPENDIX B

THE SILVER RAIL

The "Star", Toronto's largest newspaper, commissioned a study of the historic Silver Rail. It appeared on April 13, 2013 in the 'Star', and may be found on its website or in the web with the url:

http://www.blogto.com/city/2013/04/a_brief_history_of_
torontos_first_cocktail_lounge/

Posted by Chris Bateman

The article on The Silver Rail, in its entirety, appears in *Memories – Volume I: Stories for My Grandchildren* by Dr. Rocco Leonard Martino (his autobiography), in Chapter Three: "Mom and Pop."

APPENDIX C

THE SILVER GOBLET AWARD

The annual Man of the Year award, co-sponsored by *Canadian Hotel & Restaurant* and *L'Hospitalité* magazines, is presented to a member of the Canadian hospitality industry for achievement in the industry and community involvement.

The prestigious Silver Goblet was awarded posthumously in 1983 to Domenic Martino for his exceptional career and his outstanding work in the community, especially for his dedication to the children of Toronto suffering from incurable diseases.

The Man of the Year award was accepted by his two sons, Drs. Jiacomo (Jack) and Rocco (Rocky) Martino in memory of their father.

HOSPITALITY UPDATE

Silver Goblet recalls past contribution

Toronto—More than 300 members of the foodservice industry were on hand when this year's Silver Goblet Award was presented in memoriam to Domenic Martino, a longtime leader in the industry.

The award presentation was followed by loud applause from those attending the Top Management Night of the Canadian Food Service Executives Association, many of whom remembered Martino's contribution to the industry and community.

His years in the industry saw him as a cook in lumber and mining camps; a chef at the Royal York and King Edward hotels; head chef at Brant's Inn and Murphy's restaurant; and founding chef at Toronto's Silver Rail restaurant. Domenic Martino died in December.

His work in the community was outstanding. Throughout the 50's, he ran weekly movies for children at the Hospital for Sick Children in Toronto, and organized and cooked Halloween and Valentine's Day dinners for children suffering from incurable diseases.

The award was accepted by Jack and Rocky Martino in memory of their father.

The annual award, co-sponsored by *Canadian Hotel & Restaurant* and *L'Hospitalité* magazines, is presented to a member of the Canadian hospitality industry for achievement in the industry and community involvement.

Rocky Martino, right, accepts this year's Silver Goblet Award in memory of his father, Domenic Martino. Making the presentation is Editor Andrew Douglas.

CANADIAN HOTEL & RESTAURANT, FEBRUARY, 1983

216

www.ingramcontent.com/pod-product-compliance
Lightning Source LLC
LaVergne TN
LVHW051506080426
835509LV00017B/1940